Sir Martin Mar----all: or, the feign'd innocence. A comedy. By Mr. Dryden.

John Dryden

Sir Martin Mar----all: or, the feign'd innocence. A comedy. By Mr. Dryden.

Dryden, John
ESTCID: T048357
Reproduction from British Library
Titlepage in red and black. In this edition headpiece to the prologue contains a book. In some copies of: 'The dramatick works of John Dryden, Esq;' vol.2, London, 1735.
London : printed for Jacob Tonson, 1735.
[7],92-166,[2]p. : ill. ; 12°

Eighteenth Century
Collections Online
Print Editions

Gale ECCO Print Editions

Relive history with *Eighteenth Century Collections Online*, now available in print for the independent historian and collector. This series includes the most significant English-language and foreign-language works printed in Great Britain during the eighteenth century, and is organized in seven different subject areas including literature and language; medicine, science, and technology; and religion and philosophy. The collection also includes thousands of important works from the Americas.

The eighteenth century has been called "The Age of Enlightenment." It was a period of rapid advance in print culture and publishing, in world exploration, and in the rapid growth of science and technology – all of which had a profound impact on the political and cultural landscape. At the end of the century the American Revolution, French Revolution and Industrial Revolution, perhaps three of the most significant events in modern history, set in motion developments that eventually dominated world political, economic, and social life.

In a groundbreaking effort, Gale initiated a revolution of its own: digitization of epic proportions to preserve these invaluable works in the largest online archive of its kind. Contributions from major world libraries constitute over 175,000 original printed works. Scanned images of the actual pages, rather than transcriptions, recreate the works *as they first appeared.*

Now for the first time, these high-quality digital scans of original works are available via print-on-demand, making them readily accessible to libraries, students, independent scholars, and readers of all ages.

For our initial release we have created seven robust collections to form one the world's most comprehensive catalogs of 18th century works.

Initial Gale ECCO Print Editions collections include:

History and Geography
Rich in titles on English life and social history, this collection spans the world as it was known to eighteenth-century historians and explorers. Titles include a wealth of travel accounts and diaries, histories of nations from throughout the world, and maps and charts of a world that was still being discovered. Students of the War of American Independence will find fascinating accounts from the British side of conflict.

Social Science

Delve into what it was like to live during the eighteenth century by reading the first-hand accounts of everyday people, including city dwellers and farmers, businessmen and bankers, artisans and merchants, artists and their patrons, politicians and their constituents. Original texts make the American, French, and Industrial revolutions vividly contemporary.

Medicine, Science and Technology

Medical theory and practice of the 1700s developed rapidly, as is evidenced by the extensive collection, which includes descriptions of diseases, their conditions, and treatments. Books on science and technology, agriculture, military technology, natural philosophy, even cookbooks, are all contained here.

Literature and Language

Western literary study flows out of eighteenth-century works by Alexander Pope, Daniel Defoe, Henry Fielding, Frances Burney, Denis Diderot, Johann Gottfried Herder, Johann Wolfgang von Goethe, and others. Experience the birth of the modern novel, or compare the development of language using dictionaries and grammar discourses.

Religion and Philosophy

The Age of Enlightenment profoundly enriched religious and philosophical understanding and continues to influence present-day thinking. Works collected here include masterpieces by David Hume, Immanuel Kant, and Jean-Jacques Rousseau, as well as religious sermons and moral debates on the issues of the day, such as the slave trade. The Age of Reason saw conflict between Protestantism and Catholicism transformed into one between faith and logic -- a debate that continues in the twenty-first century.

Law and Reference

This collection reveals the history of English common law and Empire law in a vastly changing world of British expansion. Dominating the legal field is the *Commentaries of the Law of England* by Sir William Blackstone, which first appeared in 1765. Reference works such as almanacs and catalogues continue to educate us by revealing the day-to-day workings of society.

Fine Arts

The eighteenth-century fascination with Greek and Roman antiquity followed the systematic excavation of the ruins at Pompeii and Herculaneum in southern Italy; and after 1750 a neoclassical style dominated all artistic fields. The titles here trace developments in mostly English-language works on painting, sculpture, architecture, music, theater, and other disciplines. Instructional works on musical instruments, catalogs of art objects, comic operas, and more are also included.

The BiblioLife Network

GUIDE TO FOLD-OUTS MAPS and OVERSIZED IMAGES

Sir MARTIN MAR-ALL;

OR, THE

Feign'd INNOCENCE.

A

COMEDY.

By Mr. DRYDEN.

LONDON

Printed for JACOB TONSON in the *Strand*,

M DCC XXXV,

PROLOGUE.

FOOLS, *which each Man meets in his Dish each Day,*
  Are yet the great Regalio's of a Play ,
In which to Poets you but just appear,
To prize that highest, which cost them so dear :
Fops in the Town more easily will pass ,
One Story makes a statutable Ass ·
But such in Plays must be much thicker sown,
Like Yolks of Egs, a Dozen beat to one
Observing Poets all their Walks invade,
As Men watch Woodcocks gliding through a Glade ;
And when they have enough for Comedy,
They stow their several Bodies in a Pye .
The Poet's but the Cook to fashion it,
For, Gallants, you your selves, have found the Wit,
To bid you welcome, would your Bounty wrong,
None welcome those who bring their Cheer along

Dramatis Perſonæ.

MEN.

Lord DARTMOUTH, in Love with Mrs. CHRISTIAN.
Mr MOODY, the Swaſh buckler.
Sir MARTIN MAR-ALL, a Fool.
WARNER, his Man.
Sir JOHN SWALLOW, a *Kentiſh* Knight.

WOMEN.

Lady DUPE, the old Lady.
Mrs CHRISTIAN, her young Niece.
Mrs MILLISENT, the Swaſh-buckler's Daughter.
ROSE, her Maid.
Mrs. PREPARATION, Woman to the old Lady.

Other Servants, Men and Women, a Carrier, Bayliffs.

The SCENE, *Covent-Garden.*

Sir MARTIN MAR-ALL.

ACT I. SCENE I.

Enter Warner *folus.*

WHERE the Devil is this Mafter of mine? he is ever out o' the way when he fhould do himfelf good! This 'tis to ferve a Coxcomb, one that has no more Brains than juft thofe I carry for him Well! of all Fops commend me to him for the greateft; he's fo opinion'd of his own Abilities, that he is ever defigning fomewhat, and yet he fows his Stratagems fo fhallow, that every Daw can pick 'em up From a plotting Fool, the Lord deliver me Here he comes. Oh! it feems his Coufin's with him, then it is not fo bad as I imagin'd

Enter Sir Martin Mar-all, *and Lady* Dupe

L *Dupe* I think 'twas well contriv'd for your Accefs, to lodge her in the fame Houfe with you

Sir *Mart* 'Tis pretty well, I muft confefs

Warn Had he plotted it himfelf, it had been admirable   [*Afide.*

L *Dupe.* For when her Father *Moody* writ to me to take him Lodgings, I fo order'd it, the Choice feem'd his, not mine.

Sir Mart I have hit of a thing my felf fometimes, when wifer Heads have mifs'd it —— But that might be meer luck.

L. Dupe. Fortune does more than Wifdom

Sir Mart Nay, for that you fhall excufe me, I will not value any Man's Fortune at a Rufh, except he have Wit and Parts to bear him out. But when do you expect 'em ?

L. Dupe This Tide will bring him from *Gravefend* You had beft let your Man go as from me, and wait them at the Stairs in *Durham-Yard.*

Sir Mart Lord, Coufin, what a-do is here with your Counfel! as though I could not have thought of that my felf I could find in my Heart not to fend him now —— ftay a little —— I could foon find out fome other way

Warn. A Minute's Stay may lofe your Bufinefs

Sir Mart Well, go then —— but you muft grant, if he had ftaid, I could have found a better way —— you grant it

L Dupe For once I will not ftand with you [*Exit* Warner*] 'Tis a fweet Gentlewoman this Mrs *Milli-fent,* if you can get her.

Sir Mart Let me alone for plotting

L Dupe But by your Favour, Sir, 'tis not fo eafy, her Father has already promis'd her. And the young Gentle-man comes up with 'em I partly know the Man —— but the old Squire is humourfome, he's ftout, and plain in Speech, and in Behaviour ; he loves none of the fine Town-Tricks of Breeding, but ftands up for the old *E-lizabeth* way in all things. This we muft work upon.

Sir Mart. Sure you think you have to deal with a Fool, Coufin?

Enter Mrs Chriftian

L. Dupe O my dear Niece, I have fome Bufinefs with you   [*Whifpers.*

Sir Mart Well, Madam, I'll take one turn here i' th' *Piazza's*; a thoufand things are hammering in this Head, 'tis a fruitful Noddle, though I fay it. [*Exit Sir* Mart.

L Dupe Go thy ways for a moft conceited Fool —— But to our Bufinefs, Coufin You are young, but I am old,

old, and have had all the Love-Experience that a difcreet Lady ought to have, and therefore let me inftruct you about the Love this rich Lord makes to you

Chr You know, Madam, he's marry'd, fo that we cannot work upon that Ground of Matrimony

L. *Dupe* But there are Advantages enough for you, if you will be wife and follow my Advice

Chr Madam, my Friends left me to your Care, therefore I will wholly follow your Counfel, with Secrefy, and Obedience.

L *Dupe* Sweet-heart, it fhall be the better for you another Day. Well then, this Lord that pretends to you is crafty and falfe, as moft Men are, efpecially in Love; —— therefore we muft be fubtle to meet with all his Plots, and have Countermines againft his Works to blow him up.

Chr. As how, Madam ?

L *Dupe.* Why, Girl, he'll make fierce Love to you, but you muft not fuffer him to ruffle you, or fteal a Kifs But you muft weep and figh, and fay you'll tell me on't, and that you will not be us'd fo, and play the Innocent juft like a Child, and feem ignorant of all.

Chr I warrant you I'll be very ignorant, Madam.

L *Dupe.* And be fure when he has tows'd you, not to appear at Supper that Night, that you may fright him.

Chr No, Madam.

L *Dupe* Thar he may think you have told me.

Chr. Ay, Madam.

L *Dupe* And keep your Chamber, and fay your Head akes

Chr O moft extreamly, Madam

L. *Dupe* And lock the Door, and admit of no Night-Vifits At Supper I'll afk where's my Coufin, and being told you are not well, I'll ftart from the Table to vifit you, defiring his Lordfhip not to incommode himfelf, for I will prefently wait on him again

Chr. But how, when you are return'd, Madam ?

L *Dupe* Then fomewhat difcompos'd, I'll fay, I doubt the Meazles or Small-Pox will feize on you, and then the Girl is fpoil'd, faying, Poor thing, her Portion is

E 5   her

her Beauty and her Virtue; and often fend to fee how you
do, by Whifpers in my Servant's Ears, and have thofe
Whifpers of your Health return'd to mine. If his Lordfhip thereupon afks how you do, I will pretend it was
fome other thing

Chr. Right, Madam, for that will bring him further in
fufpence

L *Dupe* A hopeful Girl then will I eat nothing that
Night, feigning my Grief for you; but keep his Lordfhip
Company at Meal, and feem to ftrive to put my Paffion
off, yet fhew it ftill by fmall Miftakes

Chr. And broken Sentences

L *Dupe* A dainty Girl! and after Supper vifit you
again, with Promife to return ftrait to his Lordfhip But
after I am gone, fend an Excufe, that I have given you
a Cordial, and mean to watch that Night in Perfon with
you

Chr His Lordfhip then will find the Prologue of his
Trouble, doubting I have told you of his ruffling

L. *Dupe* And more than that, fearing his Father
fhould know of it, and his Wife, who is a termagant
Lady But when he finds the Coaft is clear, and his late
ruffling known to none but you, he will be drunk with
Joy

Chr Finding my fimple Innocence, which will in-
flame him more

L *Dupe* Then what the Lion's Skin has fail'd him
in, the Fox's Subtlety muft next fupply, and that is juft,
Sweet-heart, as I would have it, for crafty Folks Trea-
ties are their Advantage Efpecially when his Paffion
muft be fatisfy'd at any rate, and you keep Shop to fet
the Price of Love So now you fee the Market is your
own.

Chr. Truly, Madam, this is very rational: and by the
Bleffing of Heav'n, upon my poor Endeavours, I do not
doubt to play my part.

L. *Dupe* My Bleffing and my Pray'rs go along with
thee.

Enter

Enter Sir John Swallow, *Mrs.* Millisent, *and* Rose *her Maid*

Chr I believe, Madam, here is the young Heiress you expect, and with her he who is to marry her.

L Dupe Howe'er I am Sir *Martin's* Friend, I must not seem his Enemy.

Sir John. Madam, this fair young Lady begs the Honour to be known to you.

Mill My Father made me hope it, Madam

L Dupe. Sweet Lady, I believe you have brought all the Freshness of the Country up to Town with you

[*They salute.*

Mill I came up, Madam, as we Country-Gentlewomen use, at an *Easter*-Term, to the destruction of Tarts and Cheese-cakes, to see a new Play, buy a new Gown, take a Turn in the Park, and so down again to sleep with my Fore-fathers

Sir John Rather, Madam, you are come up to the breaking of many a poor Heart, that like mine will languish for you

Chr I doubt, Madam, you are indispos'd with your Voyage, will you please to see the Lodgings your Father has provided for you?

Mill To wait upon you, Madam

L. Dupe This is the Door —— there is a Gentleman will wait you immediately in your Lodging, if he might presume on your Commands [*In Whisper*

Mill You mean Sir *Martin Mar-all* I am glad he has entrusted his Passion with so discreet a Person

[*In whisper*

L Dupe Sir *John*, let me intreat you to stay here, that my Father may have Intelligence where to find us.

Sir John I shall obey you, Madam. [*Exe Woman.*

Enter Sir Martin Mar-all

Sir John Sir *Martin Mar-all* ! most happily encounter'd ! how long have you been come to Town ?

Sir Mart Some three Days since, or thereabouts : But I thank God I am very weary on't already.

Sir John. Wny, what's the matter, Man ?

Sir

Sir Mart. My villainous old Luck ftill follows me in Gaming, I never throw the Dice out of my Hand, but my Gold goes after 'em If I go to Picquet, though it be but with a Novice in't, he will picque and repicque, and capot me twenty times together And which moft mads me, I lofe all my Sets when I want but one of up.

Sir John. The Pleafure of Play is loft, when one lofes at that unreafonable Rate.

Sir Mart But I have fworn not to touch either Cards or Dice this half Year.

Sir John The Oaths of lofing Gamefters are moft minded, they forfwear Play as an angry Servant does his Miftrefs, becaufe he loves her but too well

Sir Mart. But I am now taken up with Thoughts of another Nature; I am in love, Sir.

Sir John That's the worft Game you could have played at, fcarce one Woman in an hundred will play with you upon the Square You venture at more Uncertainty than at a Lottery For you fet your Heart to a whole Sex of Blanks But is your Miftrefs Widow, Wife, or Maid?

Sir Mart I can affure you, Sir, mine is a Maid, the Heirefs of a wealthy Family, fair to a Miracle

Sir John. Does fhe accept your Service?

Sir Mart I am the only Perfon in her Favour.

Enter Warner

Sir John Is fhe of Town or Country?
Warn How's this?   [*Afide.*
Sir Mart She is of *Kent,* near *Canterbury*
Warn What does he mean? This is his Rival' ——
                                                      [*Afide.*

Sir John. Near *Canterbury,* fay you? I have a fmall Eftate lies thereabouts, and more Concernments than one befides

Sir Mart I'll tell you then, being at *Canterbury,* it was my Fortune once in the Cathedral Church ——

Warn What do you mean, Sir, to intruft this Man with your Affairs thus? ——————

Sir Mart Truft him? why, he's a Friend of mine.

Warn No matter for that; hark you a Word, Sir ——
                                                      Sir

Sir Mart. Pr'ythee leave fooling —— and as I was saying —— I was in the Church when I firft faw this Fair one.

Sir John Her Name, Sir, I befeech you.

Warn For Heav'n's fake, Sir, have a care

Sir Mart Thou art fuch a Coxcomb — Her Name's *Millifent*

Warn. Now, the Pox take you, Sir, what do you mean?

Sir John. Millifent, fay you? That's the Name of my Miftrefs.

Sir Mart Lord! what Luck is that now! well, Sir, it happen'd one of her Gloves fell down, I ftoop'd to take it up, and in the ftooping made her a Compliment——

Warn The Devil cannot hold him; now will this thick-skull'd Mafter of mine tell the whole Story to his Rival ——

Sir Mart You'll fay, 'twas ftrange, Sir; but at the firft Glance we caft on one another, both our Hearts leap'd within us, our Souls met at our Eyes, and with a tickling kind of Pain flid to each other's Breaft, and in one Moment fettled as clofe and warm, as if they long had been acquainted with their Lodging I follow'd her fomewhat at a diftance, becaufe her Father was with her

Warn Yet hold, Sir ——

Sir Mart Sawcy Rafcal, avoid my Sight, muft you tutor me? —— So, Sir, not to trouble you, I enquir'd out her Father's Houfe, without whofe Knowledge I did court the Daughter, and both then and often fince coming to *Canterbury*, I receiv'd many Proofs of her Kindnefs to me

Warn You had beft tell him too, that I am acquainted with her Maid, and manage your Love under-hand with her

Sir Mart Well remember'd i'faith, I thank thee for that, I had forgot it I proteft! — My *Valet de Chambre*, whom you fee here with me, grows me acquainted with her Woman ——

Warn O the Devil! ——

Sir Mart. In fine, Sir, this Maid being much in her Miſtreſs's Favour, ſo well ſollicited my Cauſe, that in fine, I gain'd from fair Miſtreſs *Milliſent* an Aſſurance of her Kindneſs, and an Engagement to marry none but me

Warn. 'Tis very well¹ you've made a fair Diſcovery¹ ——

Sir John A moſt pleaſant Relation, I aſſure you You are a happy Man, Sir¹ but, what occaſion brought you now to *London?*

Sir Mart. That was in Expectation to meet my Miſtreſs here; ſhe writ me word from *Canterbury*, ſhe and her Father ſhortly would be here

Sir John She and her Father, ſaid you, Sir?

Warn Te'l him, Sir, for Heav'n's ſake tell him all——

Sir Mart. So I will, Sir, without your bidding ——Her Father and ſhe are come up already, that's the Truth on't, and are to lodge by my Contrivance in yon Houſe, the Maſter of which is a cunning Raſcal as any in Town ——him I have made my own, for I lodge there

Warn You do ill, Sir, to ſpeak ſo ſcandalouſly of my Landlord

Sir Mart Peace, or I'll break your Fool's Head——So, that by his Means I ſhall have free Egreſs and Regreſs when I pleaſe, Sir —— without her Father's Knowledge

Warn I am out of Patience to hear this ————

Sir John Methinks you might do well, Sir, to ſpeak openly to her Father.

Sir Mart Thank you for that i'faith, in ſpeaking to old *Moody* I may ſoon ſpoil all.

Warn. So, now he has told her Father's Name, 'tis paſt Recovery.

Sir John Is her Father's Name *Moody*, ſay you?

Sir Mart Is he of your Acquaintance?

Sir John Yes, Sir, I know him for a Man who is too wiſe for you to over-reach; I am certain he will never marry his Daughter to you

Sir Mart Why, there's the Jeſt on't: He ſhall never know it 'Tis but your keeping of my Counſel, I'll do as much for you mun ——

Sir John No, Sir, I'll give you better; trouble not your ſelf about this Lady, her Affections are otherwiſe engaged,

engaged, to my Knowledge——hark in your Ear——
her Father hates a Gamester like a Devil I'll keep
your Counsel for that too

Sir *Mart* Nay, but this is not all, dear Sir *John*

Sir *John* This is all, I assure you. Only I will make
bold to seek your Mistress out another Lodging

[*Exit Sir* John.

Warn Your Affairs are now put into an excellent Po-
sture, thank your incomparable Discretion——this was a
Stratagem my shallow Wit could ne'er have reach'd, to
make a Confident of my Rival

Sir *Mart* I hope thou art not in earnest, Man! Is he
my Rival?

Warn. 'Slife he has not found it out all this while!
Well, Sir, for a quick Apprehension let you alone

Sir *Mart.* How the Devil cam'st thou to know on't?
and why the Devil didst thou not tell me on't?

Warn To the first of your Devils I answer, her Maid
Rose told me on't To the second, I wish a thousand
Devils take him that would not hear me

Sir *Mart* O unparallell'd Misfortune!

Warn O unparallell'd Ignorance! why he left her Father at the Water-side, while he led the Daughter to her
Lodging, whither I directed him, so that if you had
not laboured to the contrary, Fortune had plac'd you in
the same House with your Mistress, without the least
Suspicion of your Rival, or of her Father But 'tis
well you have satisfy'd your talkative Humour I hope
you have some new Project of your own to set all right
again · For my part, I confess all my Designs for you
are wholly ruin'd; the very Foundations of 'em are
blown up.

Sir *Mart* Pr'ythee insult not over the Destiny of a
poor undone Lover, I am punish'd enough for my In-
discretion in my Despair, and have nothing to hope
for now but Death

Warn Death is a Bug-word, things are not brought
to that Extremity, I'll cast about to save all yet

Enter

Enter Lady Dupe

L. Dupe O, Sir *Martin!* yonder has been such a stir within; Sir *John*, I fear, smokes your Design, and by all means would have the old Man remove his Lodging, pray God your Man has not play'd false.

Warn. Like enough I have: I am Coxcomb sufficient to do it; my Master knows that none but such a great Calf as I could have done it, such an overgrown Ass, a self-conceited Ideot as I——

Sir Mart Nay, *Warner*——

Warn Pray, Sir, let me alone——what is it to you if I rail upon my self? Now could I break my own Logger-head.

Sir Mart Nay, sweet *Warner*

Warn What a good Master have I, and I to ruin him : O Beast!——

L. Dupe Not to discourage you wholly, Sir *Martin*, this Storm is partly over.

Sir Mart. As how, dear Cousin?

L Dupe When I heard Sir *John* complain of the Landlord, I took the first hint of it, and join'd with him, saying, if he were such an one, I would have nothing to do with him In short I rattled him so well, that Sir *John* was the first who did desire they might be lodg'd with me, not knowing that I was your Kinswoman.

Sir Mart Pox on't, now I think on't, I could have found out this my self

Warn. Are you there again. Sir?—— now as I have a Soul——

Sir Mart Mum, good *Warner*, I did but forget my self a little, I leave my self wholly to you, and my Cousin, get but my Mistress for me, and Claim whate'er Reward you can desire

Warn Hope of Reward will Diligen beget
Find you the Mony, and I'll find the Wit.   [*Exeunt*

A C T

ACT II. SCENE I.

Enter Lady Dupe, *and Mrs* Chriſtian.

Chr IT happen'd, Madam, juſt as you ſaid it would; but was he ſo concern'd for my feign'd Sickneſs?

L *Dupe* So much that *Moody* and his Daughter, our new Gueſts, take notice of the Trouble, but the Cauſe was kept too cloſe for Strangers to divine

Chr Heav'n grant he be but deep enough in Love, and then ——

L. *Dupe* And then thou ſhalt diſtil him into Gold, my Girl Yonder he comes, I'll not be ſeen. —— you know your Leſſon, Child.   (*Exit.*

Chr. I warrant you

Enter Lord Dartmouth

Lord. Pretty Miſtreſs *Chriſtian*, how glad am I to meet you thus alone!

Chr O the Father! what will become of me now?

Lord No harm I warrant you, but why are you ſo afraid?

Chr A poor weak innocent Creature as I am, Heav'n of his Mercy, how I quake and tremble! I have not yet claw'd off your laſt ill Uſage, and now I feel my old Fit come again, my Ears tingle already, and my Back ſhuts and opens, ay, juſt ſo it began before.

Lord Nay, my ſweet Miſtreſs, be not ſo unjuſt to ſuſpect any new Attempt; I am too penitent for my laſt Fault, ſo ſoon to ſin again. —— I hope you did not tell it to your Aunt

Chr The more Fool I, I did not.

Lord You never ſhall repent your Goodneſs to me; but may not I preſume there was ſome little Kindneſs in it, which mov'd you to conceal my Crime?

Chr Methought I would not have my Aunt angry with you, for all this earthly Good, but yet I'll never be alone with you again.

Lord.

Lord. Pretty Innocence! let me fit nearer to you. You do not underftand what Love I bear you. I vow it is fo pure —— My Soul's not fully'd with one Spot of Sin. Were you a Sifter, or a Daughter to me, with a more holy Flame I could not burn

Chr. Nay, now you fpeak high Words —— I cannot underftand you

Lord The Bufinefs of my Life fhall be but how to make your Fortune, and my Care and Study to advance and fee you fettled in the World

Chr I humbly thank your Lordfhip

Lord Thus I would facrifice my Life and Fortunes, and in return you cruelly deftroy me

Chr I never meant you any harm, not I

Lord. Then what does this white Enemy fo near me? [*Touching her Hand glov'd*] Sure 'tis your Champion, and you arm it thus to bid defiance to me

Chr. Nay, fie my Lord, in faith you are to blame
                              [*Pulling her Hand away.*

Lord. But I am for fair Wars, an Enemy muft firft be fearch'd for privy Armour ere we do ingage.
                              [*Pulls at her Glove.*

Chr. What does your Lordfhip mean?

Lord. I fear you bear fome Spells and Charms about you, and, Madam, that's againft the Law of Arms

Chr. My Aunt charg'd me not to pull off my Glove for fear of Sun-burning my Hand

Lord She did well to keep it from your Eyes, but I will thus preferve it   [*Hugging her bare Hand*

Chr Why do you crufh it fo? nay, now you hurt me, nay —— if you fqueeze it ne'er fo hard —— there's nothing to come out on't —— fie —— is this loving one —— What makes you take your Breath fo fhort?

Lord The Devil take me if I can anfwer her a Word, all my Senfes are quite imploy'd another way

Chr. Ne'er ftir, my Lord, I muft cry out ——

Lord Then I muft ftop your Mouth —— this Ruby for a Kifs —— that is but one Ruby for another.

Chr. This is worfe and worfe.

Lady within. Why Niece, where are you, Niece?
                              Lord.

Lord. Pox of her old mouldy ·Chops.

Chr Do you hear, my Aunt calls? I shall be hang'd for staying with you — let me go, my Lord. [*Gets from him.*

Enter Lady Dupe.

L *Dupe* My Lord, Heav'n bless me, what makes your Lordship here?

Lord I was just wishing for you, Madam; your Niece and I have been so laughing at the blunt Humour of your Country-Gentleman —— I must go pass an Hour with him [*Exit Lord.*

Chr. You made a little too much haste; I was just exchanging a Kiss for a Ruby

L *Dupe.* No harm done; it will make him come on the faster Never full-gorge an Hawk you mean to fly: The next will be a Neck-lace of Pearl, I warrant you.

Chr. But what must I do next?

L *Dupe* Tell him I grew suspicious, and examin'd you whether he made not Love; which you deny'd. Then tell him how my Maids and Daughters watch you; so that you tremble when you see his Lordship.

Chr. And·that your Daughters are so envious, that they would raise a false Report to ruin me.

L. *Dupe.* Therefore you desire his Lordship, as he Loves you, of which you are confident, hence-forward to forbear his Visits to you.

Chr But how, if he should take me at my Word?

L *Dupe* Why, if the worst come to the worst, he leaves you an honest Woman, and there's an end on't: But fear not that, hold out his Messages, and then he'll write, and that is it, my Bird, which you must drive it to · Then all his Letters will be such Ecstasies, such Vows and Promises, which you must answer short and simply, yet still ply out of 'em your Advantages

Chr But, Madam! he's i'th' House, he will not write

L. *Dupe.* You Fool —— he'll write from the next Chamber to you. And rather than fail, send his Page Post with it upon a Hobby-horse —— Then grant a Meeting, but tell me of it, and I'll prevent him by my being there, he'll curse me, but I care not When you

are

are alone, he'll urge his Luſt, which anſwer you with Scorn and Anger. ⸺

Chr As thus, an't pleaſe you, Madam What? Does he think I will be damn'd for him? Defame my Family, ruin my Name, to ſatisfie his Pleaſure?

L. Dupe Then he will be prophane in's Arguments, urge Nature's Laws to you.

Chr By'r Lady, and thoſe are ſhrewd Arguments, but I am reſolv'd I'll ſtop my Ears

L. Dupe Then when he ſees no other thing will move you, he'll ſign a Portion to you beforehand Take hold of that, and then of what you will. [*Exeunt*

Enter *Sir* John, *Mrs* Milliſent, *and* Roſe.

Sir John Now, fair Mrs. *Milliſent*, you ſee your Chamber, your Father will be buſie a few Minutes, and in the mean time permits me the Happineſs to wait on you. ⸺

Mill. Methinks you might have choſe us better Lodgings, this Houſe is full; the other we ſaw firſt, was more convenient

Sir John For you perhaps, but not for me. You might have met a Lover there, but I a Rival.

Mill What Rival?

Sir John. You know Sir *Martin*, I need not name it to you

Mill I know more Men beſides him.

Sir John. But you love none beſides him Can you deny your Affection to him?

Mill You have vex'd me ſo, I will not ſatisfie you.

Sir John Then I perceive I am not likely to be ſo much oblig'd to you, as I was to him

Mill. This is Romance, ⸺ I'll not believe a word on't. ⸺

Sir John. That's as you pleaſe: However 'tis believ'd, his Wit will not much credit your Choice. Madam, do juſtice to us both; pay his Ingratitude and Folly with your Scorn; my Service with your Love By this time your Father ſtays for me. I ſhall be diſcreet enough to keep this Fault of yours from him, the Lawyers wait for us to draw your Jointure: And I would beg your
Pardon

Pardon for my Abſence, but that my Crime is puniſh'd in it ſelf.   [*Exit.*

Mill. Could I ſuſpect this Uſage from a favour'd Serꝟant!

Roſe. Firſt hear Sir *Martin,* ere you quite condemn him; conſider 'tis a Rival who accus'd him.

Mill Speak not a word in his behalf · — Methought too, Sir *John* call'd him Fool.

Roſe. Indeed he has a rare way of acting a Fool, and does it ſo naturally, it can be ſcarce diſtinguiſh'd.

Mill. Nay he has Wit enough, that's certain

Roſe. How blind Love is!

Enter Warner

Mill. How now, what's his Buſineſs? I wonder after ſuch a Crime, if his Maſter has the face to ſend him to me.

Roſe How durſt you venture hither? If either Sir *John* or my old Maſter ſee you ————

Warn. Piſh! they are both gone out.

Roſe They went but to the next Street; ten to one but they return and catch you here.

Warn. Twenty to one I am gone before, and ſave em a labour

Mill What ſays that Fellow to you? What Buſineſs can he have here?

Warn Lord, that your Ladyſhip ſhould ask that Queſtion, knowing whom I ſerve!

Mill I'll hear nothing from your Maſter

Warn. Never breathe, but this Anger becomes your Ladyſhip moſt admirably; but though you'll hear nothing from him, I hope I may ſpeak a word or two to you from my ſelf, Madam.

Roſe. 'Twas a ſweet Prank your Maſter play'd us. A Lady's well helpt up that truſts her Honour in ſuch a Perſon's Hands. To tell all ſo, ———— and to his Rival too   Excuſe him if thou canſt   [*Aſide.*

Warn How the Devil ſhould I excuſe him? Thou know'ſt he is the greateſt Fop in Nature————

[*Aſide to* Roſe.

Roſe But my Lady does not know it; if ſhe did—

Mill. I'll have no whiſpering.

Wam.

Warn. Alas, Madam, I have not the Confidence to speak out, unless you can take Mercy on me.

Mill. For what?

Warn. For telling Sir *John* you lov'd my Master, Madam. But sure I little thought he was his Rival.

Rose The witty Rogue has taken't on himself. [*Aside.*

Mill. Your Master then is innocent?

Warn. Why, could your Ladyship suspect him guilty? Pray tell me, do you think him ungrateful, or a Fool?

Mill. I think him neither

Warn. Take it from me, you see not the Depth of him. But when he knows what Thoughts you harbour of him, as I am faithful, and must tell him —— I wish he does not take pet, and leave you

Mill. Thou art not mad, I hope, to tell him on't, if thou dost, I'll be sworn I'll forswear it to him

Warn Upon Condition then you'll pardon me, I'll see what I can do to hold my Tongue

Mill. This Evening in St. *James*'s Park I'll meet him. [*Knock within*

Warn. He shall not fail you, Madam

Rose Some Body knocks — Oh, Madam, what shall we do ! 'tis Sir *John*, I hear his Voice.

Warn. What will become of me?

Mill. Step quickly behind that Door. [*Warner goes out.*

To them Sir John

Mill You've made a quick dispatch, Sir.

Sir John We have done nothing, Madam, our Man of Law was not within —— but I must look some Writings.

Mill Where are they laid?

Sir John. In the Portmanteau in the Drawing-Room. [*Is going to the Door.*

Mill. Pray stay a little, Sir ——

Warn [*At the Door*] He must pass just by me; and if he sees me, I am but a dead Man.

Sir John. Why are you thus concern'd? why do you hold me?

Mill. Only a Word or two I have to tell you. 'Tis of Importance to you ——

Sir John. Give me leave ——   *Mill.*

Mill I muſt not, before I diſcover the Plot to you.

Sir *John* What Plot?

Mill Sir *Martin*'s Servant, like a Rogue, comes hither to tempt me, from his Maſter, to have met him

Warn [*At the Door*] Now would I had a good Bag of Gun-powder at my Breech, to ram me into ſome Hole.

Mill. For my part I was ſo ſtartled at the Meſſage, that I ſhall ſcarcely be my ſelf theſe two Days.

Sir *John* Oh that I had the Raſcal! I would teach him to come upon ſuch Errands.

Warn Oh for a gentle Compoſition now! an Arm or Leg I would give willingly

Sir *John.* What Anſwer did you make the Villain?

Mill. I over-reach'd him clearly, by a Promiſe of an Appoinment of a Place I nam'd, where I ne'er meant to come. But would have had the Pleaſure firſt to tell you how I ſerv'd him

Sir *John.* And then to chide your mean Suſpicion of me, indeed I wonder'd you ſhould love a Fool. But where did you appoint to meet him?

Mill In *Grays-Inn* Walks

Warn By this Light, ſhe has put the Change upon him! O ſweet Woman-kind, how I love thee for that heav'nly Gift of Lying!

Sir *John.* For this Evening I will be his Miſtreſs; he ſhall meet another *Penelope* than he ſuſpects.

Mill But ſtay not long away.

Sir *John.* You over-joy me, Madam   [*Exit.*

Warn [*Entring*] Is he gone, Madam?

Mill. As far as *Grays-Inn* Walks. Now I have time to walk the other way, and ſee thy Maſter.

Warn Rather let him come hither. I have laid a Plot ſhall ſend his Rival far enough from watching him ere long

Mill Art thou in earneſt?

Warn 'Tis ſo deſign'd, Fate cannot hinder it. Our Landlord where we lie, vex'd that his Lodgings ſhould be ſo left by Sir *John*, is reſolv'd to be reveng'd, and I have found the way You'll ſee th' effect on't preſently.

Roſe. O Heav'ns! the Door opens again, and Sir *John* is return'd once more,   *Enter*

Enter Sir John.

Sir John Half my Bufinefs was forgot; you did not tell me when you were to meet him. Ho! What makes this Rafcal here?

Warn 'Tis well you're come, Sir, elfe I muft have left untold a Meffage I have for you.

Sir John Well, what's your Bufinefs, Sirrah?

Warn. We muft be private firft; 'tis only for your Ear.

Rofe. I fhall admire his Wit, if in this plunge he can get off

Warn I came hither, Sir, by my Mafter's Order —

Sir John I'll reward you for it, Sirrah, immediately

Warn. When you know all, I fhall deferve it, Sir, I came to found the Virtue of your Miftrefs; which I have done fo cunningly, I have at laft obtain'd the Promife of a Meeting But my good Mafter, whom I muft confefs more generous than wife, knowing you had a Paffion for her, is refolv'd to quit: And, Sir, that you may fee how much he loves you, fent me in private to advife you ftill to have an Eye upon her Actions.

Sir John. Take this Diamond for thy good News; and give thy Mafter my Acknowledgments

Warn Thus the World goes, my Mafters, he that will cozen you, commonly gets your Good will into the Bargain. [*Afide*

Sir John Madam, I am now fatisfy'd of all fides, firft of your Truth, then of Sir *Martin*'s Friendfhip In fhort, I find you two cheated each other, both to be true to me.

Mill. Warner is got off as I would wifh, and the Knight over-reach'd

Enter to them the Landlord difguis'd like a Carrier.

Rofe How now! what would this Carrier have?

Warn This is our Landlord whom I told you of; but keep your Countenance ———— [*Afide to her.*

Land I was looking here-away for one Sir *John Swallow*; they told me I might hear News of him in this Houfe.

Sir

Sir John. Friend, I am the Man, What have you to say to me?

Land Nay, Faith Sir, I am not so good a Schollard to say much, but I have a Letter for you in my Pouch: There's plaguy News in it, I can tell you that.

Sir John From whom is your Letter?

Land From your old Uncle *Anthony*

Sir John. Give me your Letter quickly.

Land Nay, soft and fair goes far —————— Hold you, hold you It is not in this Pocket.

Sir John. Search in the other then, I stand on Thorns.

Land I think I feel it now, this should be who

Sir John. Pluck it out then

Land I'll pluck out my Spectacles and see first [*Reads*] To Mr *Paul Grimbard* ——— Apprentice to ——— No, that's not for you, Sir, ——— that's for the Son of the Brother of the Nephew of the Cousin of my Gossip *Dobson*

Sir John Pr'ythee dispatch, do'st thou not know the Contents on't?

Land Yes, as well as I do my *Pater Noster*

Sir John. Well, what's the Business on't?

Land Nay, no great Business; 'tis but only that your Worship's Father's dead

Sir John. My Loss is beyond Expression! how dy'd he?

Land. He went to Bed as well to see to as any Man in *England,* and when he awaken'd the next Morning ———

Sir John What then?

Land. He found himself stark dead

Sir John Well, I must of necessity take orders for my Father's Funeral, and my Estate, Heav'n knows with what Regret I leave you, Madam

Mill But are you in such haste, Sir? I see you take all occasions to be from me.

Sir John. Dear Madam, say not so; a few Days will, I hope, return me to you

To them Sir Martin

Noble Sir *Martin,* the welcomest Man alive! let me embrace my Friend.

Rose. How untowardly he returns the Salute! *Warner* will be found out   [*Aside*

Sir John. Well Friend! you have oblig'd me to you eternally.

Sir Mart. How have I oblig'd you, Sir? I would have you to know I scorn your Words; and I would I were hang'd, if it be not the farthest off my Thoughts.

Mill. O cunning Youth, he acts the Fool most naturally. Were we alone, how would we laugh together!   [*Aside.*

Sir John. This is a double Generosity, to do me Favours, and conceal 'em from me, but honest *Warner* here has told me all

Sir Mart. What has the Rascal told you?

Sir John. Your Plot to try my Mistress for me —— you understand me, concerning your Appointment

Warn. Sir, I desire to speak in private with you

Sir Mart. This impertinent Rascal, when I am most busy, I am ever troubled with him

Warn. But it concerns you I should speak with you, good Sir

Sir Mart. That's a good one i'faith, thou know'st Breeding well, that I should whisper with a Serving-man before Company

Warn. Remember, Sir, last time it had been better ——

Sir Mart. Peace, or I'll make you feel my double Fists; if I don't fright him, the sawcy Rogue will call me Fool before the Company

Mill. That was acted most naturally again   [*Aside.*

Sir John. [*To him*] But what needs this dissembling, since you are resolv'd to quit my Mistress to me?

Sir Mart. I quit my Mistress! that's a good one i'faith.

Mill. Tell him you have forsaken me   [*Aside.*

Sir Mart. I understand you, Madam, you would save a Quarrel, but i'faith I'm not so base   I'll see him hang'd first

Warn. Madam, my Master is convinc'd, in Prudence he should say so   But Love o'ermasters him, when you are gone perhaps he may

Mill. I'll go then   Gentlemen, your Servant, I see my Presence brings constraint to the Company

[*Exeunt Mill and Rose*
Sir John.

Sir John I'm glad fhe's gone , now we may talk more freely ; for if you have not quitted her, you muft

Warn. Pray, Sir, remember your felf, did not you fend me of a Meffage to Sir *John*, that for his Friendfhip you had left Miftrefs *Millifent?*

Sir Mart Why, what an impudent lying Rogue art thou!

Sir John How's this! has *Warner* cheated me?

Warn Do not fufpect it in the leaft You know, Sir, it was not generous before a Lady, to fay he quitted her

Sir John O! was that it?

Warn That was all Say Yes, good Sir *John* —— or I'll fwinge you! [*Afide.*

Sir Mart. Yes, good Sir *John*.

Warn That's well, once in his Life he has heard good Counfel.

Sir Mart Heigh, heigh, what makes my Landlord here? he has put on a Fool's Coat, I think, to make us laugh.

Warn The Devil's in him, he's at it again, his Folly's like a Sore in a furfeited Horfe, cure it in one Place, and it breaks out in another.

Sir Mart Honeft Landlord i'faith, and what makes you here?

Sir John Are you acquainted with this honeft Man?

Land Take heed what you fay, Sir [*To Sir* Mart *foftly*

Sir Mart Take heed what you fay, Sir! why? whom fhould I be afraid of? of you, Sir? I fay, Sir, I know him, Sir, and I have reafon to know him, Sir, for I am fure I lodge in his Houfe, Sir —— nay, never think to ter-rify me, Sir, 'tis my Landlord here in *Charles-ftreet*, Sir

Land Now I expect to be paid for the News I brought him

Sir John Sirrah, did not you tell me that my Father ---

Land Is in very good Health, for ought I know, Sir, I befeech you to trouble your felf no farther concerning him

Sir John Who fet you on to tell this Lye?

Sir Mart. Ay, who fet you on, Sirrah? This was a Rogue that would cozen us both; he thought I did not know him Down on your Marrowbones, and confefs the Truth. Have you no Tongue, you Rafcal?

Sir John Sure 'tis fome filenc'd Minifter He grows fo fat he cannot fpeak

Land Why, Sir, if you would know, 'twas for your sake I did it

Warn For my Master's sake! why, you impudent Varlet, do you think to 'scape us with a Lye?

Sir John How was it for his sake?

Warn 'Twas for his own, Sir, he heard you were th' occasion the Lady lodg'd not at his House, and so he invented this Lye, partly to revenge himself of you; and partly, I believe, in hope to get her once again when you were gone

Sir John Fetch me a Cudgel pr'ythee

Land O good Sir! if you beat me I shall run into Oil immediately.

Warn Hang him Rogue, he's below your Anger I'll maul him for you ———— the Rogue's so big, I think 'twill ask two Days to beat him all over   [*Beats him*

Land. O Rogue, O Villain *Warner!* bid him hold and I'll confess, Sir

Warn Get you gone without replying. Must such as you be prating?   [*Beats him out*

Enter Rose

Rose Sir, Dinner waits you on the Table

Sir John Friend, will you go along, and take part of a bad Repast?

Sir Mart Thank you; but I am just risen from Table

Warn Now he might sit with his Mistress, and has not the Wit to find it out

Sir John You shall be very welcome

Sir Mart I have no Stomach, Sir

Warn Get you in with a Vengeance· You have a better Stomach than you think you have   [*Pushes him*

Sir Mart This hungry *Diego* Rogue would shame me; he thinks a Gentleman can eat like a Serving-man

Sir John If you will not, adieu, dear Sir, in any thing command me   [*Exit*

Sir Mart. Now we are alone, han't I carry'd Matters bravely, Sirrah?

Warn O yes, yes, you deserve Sugar-plums, first for your quarrelling with Sir *John*; then for discovering your Landlord, and lastly for refusing to dine with your Mistress. All this is since the last Reckoning was wip'd out.

Sir *Mart.*

Sir Mart Then why did my Landlord difguife himfelf, to make a Fool of us?

Warn. You have fo little Brains, that a Penn'orth of Butter melted under 'em, would fet 'em afloat. He put on that Difguife, to rid you of your Rival

Sir Mart Why was not I worthy to keep your Counfel then?

Warn. It had been much at one. You would but have drunk the Secret down, and pifs'd it out to the next Company

Sir Mart Well, I find I am a miferable Man. I have loft my Miftrefs, and may thank my felf for't

Warn You'll not confefs you are a Fool, I warrant

Sir Mart Well I am a Fool, if that will fatisfy you. But what am I the nearer for being one?

Warn O yes, much the nearer; for now Fortune's bound to provide for you, as Hofpitals are built for lame People, becaufe they cannot help themfelves. Well, I have a Project in my Pate

Sir Mart Dear Rogue, what is't?

Warn Excufe me for that. But while 'tis fet a working, you would do well to fcrue your felf into her Father's good Opinion

Sir Mart If you will not tell me, my Mind gives me I fhall difcover it again

Warn I'll lay it as far out of your reach as I can poffibly

———— For Secrets are edg'd Tools,
And muft be kept from Children and from Fools. [*Exit*

ACT III. SCENE I.

Enter Rose *and* Warner *meeting.*

Rose. YOur Worfhip's moft happily encounter'd.

    Warn Your Ladyfhip's moft fortunately met.

Rose I was going to your Lodging.

Warn. My Bufinefs was to yours

Rose I have fomething to fay to you that——

Warn I have that to tell you——

Rose Underftand then——

Warn If you'll hear me——

Rose I believe that——

Warn. I am of Opinion, that——

Rose Pr'ythee hold thy Peace a little, till I have done.

Warn Cry you Mercy, Miftrefs *Rose,* I'll not difpute your ancient Privileges of talking.

Rose My Miftrefs, knowing Sir *John* was to be abroad upon Bufinefs this Afternoon, has afked leave to fee a Play and Sir *John* has fo great a Confidence of your Mafter, that he will truft no Body with her, but him

Warn If my Mafter gets her out, I warrant her, he fhall fhow her a better Play than any is at either of the Houfes —— here they are . I'll run and prepare him to wait upon her   [*Exit.*

    Enter old Moody, *Mis* Millifent, *and Lady* Dupe.

Mill My Hood and Scarfs there, quickly

L. Dupe. Send to call a Coach there

Mood But what kind of Man is this Sir *Martin,* with whom you are to go ?

L Dupe A plain down-right Country Gentleman, I affure you

                                    Mood.

Mood. I like him much the better for't For I hate one of thofe you call a Man o' th' Town, one of thofe empty Fellows of meer Out-fide : They've nothing of the true old *Englifh* Manlinefs

Rofe I confefs, Sir, a Woman's in a bad Condition, that has nothing to truft to, but a Peruke above, and a well-trim'd Shoe below

To them Sir Martin

Mill This, Sir, is Sir *John's* Friend, he is for your Humour, Sir, he is no Man o' th' Town, but bred up in the old *Elizabeth* Way of Plainnefs

Sir Mart Ay, Madam, your Ladyfhip may fay your Pleafure of me.

To them Warner.

Warn How the Devil got he here before me ! 'I'm very unlucky I could not fee him firft ————

Sir Mart. But, as for Painting, Mufick, Poetry, and the like, I'll fay this of my felf ————

Warn I'll fay that for him, my Mafter underftands none of 'em, I affure you, Sir

Sir Mart. You impudent Rafcal, hold your Tongue. I muft rid my Hands of this Fellow; the Rogue is ever difcrediting me before Company.

Mood Never trouble your felf about it, Sir, for I like a Man that ————

Sir Mart I know you do, Sir, and therefore I hope you'll think never the worfe of me for his praifing For, though I do not boaft of my own good Parts ————

Warn He has none to boaft of, upon my Faith, Sir.

Sir Mart. Give him not the Hearing, Sir ; for, if I may believe my Friends, they have flatter'd me with an Opinion of more ————

Warn Of more than their Flattery can make good, Sir ; ———— 'tis true he tells you, they have flatter'd him ; but, in my Confcience, he is the moft downright fimple-natur'd Creature in the World

Sir Mart I fhall confider you hereafter, Sirrah, but I am fure in all Companies I pafs for a *Vertuofo.*

Mood Vertuofo ! What's that too ? is not *Vertue* enough without *O fo ?*

F 4 *Sir*

Sir Mart You have Reafon, Sir!

Mood. There he is again too; the Town Phrafe, a great Compliment I wifs, you have Reafon, Sir, that is, you are no Beaft, Sir.

Warn A Word in private, Sir; you miftake this old Man; he loves neither Painting, Mufick, nor Poetry, yet recover your felf, if you have any Brains

[*Afide to him*

Sir Mart Say you fo? I'll bring all about again I warrant you —— I beg your Pardon a thoufand times, Sir; I vow to gad I am not Mafter of any of thofe Perfections, for, in fine, Sir, I am wholly ignorant of Painting, Mufick, and Poetry, only fome rude E-fcapes —— but, in fine, they are fuch, that, in fine, Sir ——

Warn. This is worfe than all the reft   [*Afide.*

Mood By Coxbones, one Word more of all this Gibberifh, and old Madge fhall fly about your Ears: What is this *in fine* he keeps fuch a Coil with too?

Mill. 'Tis a Phrafe *a-la-mode*, Sir, and is us'd in Converfation now, as a Whiff of Tobacco was formerly in the midft of a Difcourfe for a thinking While.

L. Dupe. In plain *Englifh, in fine, is, In the end,* Sir

Mood. But by Coxbones there is no end on't me-thinks. If thou wilt have a foolifh Word to lard thy lean Difcourfe with, take an *Englifh* one when thou fpeakeft *Englifh!* as, So Sir, And then Sir, And fo forth; 'tis a more manly kind of Nonfenfe And a Pox of *in fine,* for I'll hear no more on't

Warn He's gravell'd, and I muft help him out.

[*Afide.*

Madam, there's a Coach at Door to carry you to the Play

Sir Mart Which Houfe do you mean to go to?

Mill The Duke's, I think.

Sir Mart. It is a damn'd Play, and has nothing in't.

Mill Then let us to the King's.

Sir Mart. That's e'en as bad.

Warn.

Warn. This is paſt enduring [*Aſide*] There was an ill Play ſet up, Sir, on the Poſts; but I can aſſure you the Bills are alter'd ſince you ſaw 'em, and now there are two admirable Comedies at both Houſes

Mood But my Daughter loves ſerious Plays

Warn They are Tragi-Comedies, Sir, for both.

Sir *Mart* I have heard her ſay, ſhe loves none but Tragedies

Mood Where have you heard her ſay ſo, Sir?

Warn Sir, you forget your ſelf, you never ſaw her in your Life before

Sir *Mart* What, not at *Canterbury*, in the Cathedral Church there? This is the impudenteſt Raſcal ———

Warn Mum, Sir ———

Sir *Mart.* Ah Lord, what have I done! As I hope to be ſav'd, Sir, it was before I was aware, for if ever I ſet Eyes on her before this Day —— I wiſh ——

Mood This Fellow is not ſo much Fool, as he makes one believe he is.

Mill. I thought he would be diſcover'd for a Wit. This 'tis to over-act one's Part! [*Aſide.*

Mood Come away Daughter, I will not truſt you in his Hands, there's more in't than I imagin'd

[*Exeunt* Moody, Mill *Lady* Dupe, *and* Roſe.

Sir *Mart* Why do you frown upon me ſo, when you know your Looks go to the Heart of me, what have I done beſides a little *lapſus Linguæ?*

Warn Why, who ſays you have done any thing? You, a meer Innocent!

Sir *Mart* As the Child that's to be born, in my Intentions, if I know how I have offended, my ſelf, any more than in one Word ———

Warn But don't follow me however —— I have nothing to ſay to you

Sir *Mart* I'll follow you to the World's End, 'till you forgive me

Warn I am reſolv'd to lead you a Dance then

[*Exit running*

Sir *Mart* The Rogue has no Mercy in him, but I muſt mollify him with Money [*Exit.*

Enter

Enter Lady Dupe

L *Dupe.* Truly my little Coufin's the apteft Scholar, and takes out Love's Leffons fo exactly, that I joy to fee it She has got already the Bond of two thoufand Pound feal'd for her Portion, which I keep for her, a pretty good Beginning: 'Tis true, I believe he has enjoy'd her, and fo let him; *Mark Anthony* woo'd not at fo dear a Price

Enter to her Chriftian.

Chr. O Madam, I fear I am breeding'

L *Dupe* A taking Wench' but 'tis no matter, have you told any Body?

Chr I have been venturing upon your Foundations, a little to diffemble

L *Dupe* That's a good Child, I hope it will thrive with thee, as it has with me Heav'n has a Bleffing in ftore upon our Endeavours

Chr I feign'd my felf fick, and kept my Bed, my Lord, he came to vifit me, and in the end I difclos'd it to him in the faddeft Paffion

L *Dupe* This frighten'd him, I hope, into a Study how to cloak your Difgrace, left it fhould have vent to his Lady

Chr 'Tis true; but all the while I fubt'ly drove it, that he fhould name you to me as the fitteft Inftrument of the Concealment; but how to break it to you, ftrangely does perplex him He has been feeking you all o'er the Houfe, therefore I'll leave your Ladyfhip, for fear we fhould be feen together   [*Exit*

L *Dupe* Now I muft play my Part ·
Nature, in Women, teaches more than Art

Enter Lord

Lord Madam, I have a Secret to impart; a fad one too, and have no Friend to truft but only you

L *Dupe* Your Lady or your Children fick?

Lord Not that I know

L *Dupe* You feem to be in Health

Lord In Body, not in Mind

L *Dupe* Some fcruple of Confcience, I warrant, my Chaplain fhall refolve you.

Lord

Lord Madam, my Soul's tormented.

L *Dupe*. O take heed of Despair, my Lord!

Lord Madam, there is no Medicine for this Sickness, but only you, your Friendship's my safe Haven, else I am lost, and Ship-wrack'd

L *Dupe*. Pray tell me what it is.

Lord. Could I express it by sad Sighs and Groans, or drown it with my self in Seas of Tears, I should be happy, would, and would not tell

L *Dupe*. Command whatever I can serve you in, I will be faithful still to all your Ends, provided they are just and virtuous.

Lord. That Word has stopt me.

L *Dupe* Speak out, my Lord, and boldly tell what 'tis

Lord Then in Obedience to your Commands; your Cousin is with Child

L *Dupe*. Which Cousin?

Lord Your Cousin *Christian*, here i' th' House

L *Dupe*. Alas! then she has stol'n a Marriage, and undone her self. Some young Fellow, on my Conscience, that's a Beggar; Youth will not be advis'd, well, I'll never meddle more with Girls; one is no more assur'd of 'em, than Grooms of Mules, they'll strike when least one thinks on't But pray your Lordship, what is her Choice then for a Husband?

Lord She is not married that I know of, Madam

L *Dupe*. Not married! 'tis impossible, the Girl does sure abuse you I know her Education has been such, the Flesh could not prevail; therefore she does abuse you, it must be so

Lord Madam, not to abuse you longer, she is with Child, and I the unfortunate Man who did this most unlucky Act

L *Dupe* You! I'll never believe it

Lord Madam, 'tis too true, believe it, and be serious how to hide her Shame; I beg it here upon my Knees

L *Dupe* Oh, oh, oh!   [*She faints away*

Lord. Who's there? Who's there? Help help, my p——

Enter

Enter two Women, Rose *and* Penelope.

1 *Wom.* O merciful God, my Lady's gone!

2 *Wom* Whither?

1 *Wom* To Heav'n, God knows to Heav'n!

Rose Rub her, rub her; fetch warm Cloaths!

2 *Wom* I say, run to the Cabinet of Quinteffence;
Gilbert's Water! *Gilbert's* Water!

1 *Wom.* Now all the good Folks of Heav'n look
down upon her.

Mill Set her in the Chair

Rose. Open her Mouth with a Dagger or a Key,
pour, pour Wher's the Spoon?

2 *Wom* She ftirs! fhe revives! merciful to us all!
what a thing was this? fpeak, Lady, fpeak!

L. Dupe So, fo, fo!

Mill Alas! my Lord, how came this Fit?

Lord With Sorrow, Madam

L. Dupe. Now I am better · *Befs,* you have not feen
me thus?

1 *Wom.* Heav'n forefend that I fhould live to fee you
fo again

L Dupe. Go, go, I'm pretty well; withdraw into
the next Room; but be near, I pray, for fear of the
worft [*They go out*] —— My Lord, fit down near me I
pray, I'll ftrive to fpeak a few Words to you, and
then to Bed —— nearer, my Voice is faint —— My
Lord, Heav'n knows how I have ever lov'd you; and,
is this my Reward? Had you none to abufe but me in
that unfortunate fond Girl, that you know was dearer to
me than my Life? This was not Love to her, but an
inveterate Malice to poor me Oh, oh. — [*Faints again.*

Lord Help, help, help!

All the Women again.

1 *Wom.* This Fit will carry her. Alas, it is a Lechery!

2 *Wom* The Balfom, the Balfom!

1 *Wom* No, no, the Chymiftry Oyl of Rofemary.
Hold her up, and give her Air.

Mill Feel whether fhe breathes, with your Hand before her Mouth

Rose.

Rose No, Madam, 'tis Key-cold

1 *Wom.* Look up, dear Madam, if you have any hope of Salvation !

2 *Wom.* Hold up your Finger, Madam, if you have any hope of Fraternity   O the bleſſed Saints that hear me not, take her Mortality to them

L *Dupe* Enough, ſo 'tis well ——— withdraw, and let me reſt a while ; only my dear Lord remain.

1 *Wom.* Pray your Lordſhip keep her from ſwebbing.

[*Exeunt Women.*]

Lord. Here humbly once again, I beg your Pardon and your Help.

L *Dupe* Heav'n forgive you, and I do . Stand up, my Lord, and ſit cloſe by me · O this naughty Girl ! but did your Lordſhip win her ſoon ?

Lord No, Madam, but with much Difficulty.

L. *Dupe.* I'm glad on't ; it ſhew'd the Girl had ſome Religion in her, all my Precepts were not in vain : But you Men are ſtrange Tempters ; good my Lord, where was this wicked Act then firſt committed ?

Lord In an Out-Room upon a Trunk.

L *Dupe* Poor Heart, what ſhift Love makes ! Oh, ſhe does love you dearly, tho' to her Ruin ! and then what Place, my Lord?

Lord An old waſte Room, with a decay'd Bed in't.

L *Dupe* Out upon that dark Room for Deeds of Darkneſs ! and that rotten Bed ! I wonder it did hold your Lordſhip's Vigour : But you dealt gently with the Girl Well, you ſhall ſee I love you· For I will manage this Buſineſs to both your Advantages, by the Aſſiſtance of Heav'n I will ; good my Lord help, lead me out   [*Exeunt.*

Enter Warner *and* Roſe

Roſe A Miſchief upon all Fools ! do you think your Maſter has not done wiſely ? Firſt to miſtake our old Man's Humour, then to diſpraiſe the Plays , and laſtly, to diſcover his Acquaintance with my Miſtreſs My old Maſter has taken ſuch a Jealouſy of him, that he will never admit him into his ſight again.

Warn Thou mak'ſt thy ſelf a greater Fool than he, by being angry at what he cannot help ——— I have been

angry

angry with him too; but these Friends have taken up the Quarrel —— [*Shews Gold*] Look you, he has sent these Mediators to mitigate your Wrath Here are twenty of 'em have made a long Voyage from *Guinea* to kiss your Hands · And when the Match is made, there are an hundred more in readiness to be your humble Servants

Rose. Rather than fall out with you, I'll take 'em; but I confess, it troubles me to see so loyal a Lover have the Heart of an Emperor, and yet scarce the Brains of a Cobler

Warn Well, what Device can we two beget betwixt us, to separate Sir *John Swallow* and thy Mistress?

Rose I cannot on the sudden tell, but I hate him worse than foul Weather without a Coach.

Warn. Then I ll see if my Project be luckier than thine. Where are the Papers concerning the Jointure I have heard you speak of?

Rose They lie within in three great Bags, some twenty Reams of Paper in each Bundle with six Lines in a Sheet. But there is a little Paper where all the Business lies.

Warn Where is it? Canst thou help me to it?

Rose. By good Chance he gave it to my Custody before he set out for *London* You came in good time, here it is, I was carrying it to him, just now he sent for it

Warn So, this I will secure in my Pocket, when thou art ask'd for it, make two or three bad Faces, and say 'twas left behind By this means, he must of Necessity leave the Town, to see for it in *Kent*

    Enter Sir John, *Sir* Martin, *Mrs* Millisent

Sir John. 'Tis no matter, though the old Man be suspicious; I knew the Story all before-hand, and since then you have fully satisfy'd me of your true Friendship to me —————— Where are the Writings?   [*To* Rose.

Rose. Sir, I beg your Pardon; I thought I had put 'em up amongst my Lady's Things, and it seems in my haste, I quite forgot 'em, and left 'em at *Canterbury*

† *Sir John* This is horribly unlucky! where do you think you left 'em?

Rose Upon the great Box in my Lady's Chamber; they are safe enough I'm sure

                                                    Sir John.

Sir John. It muſt be ſo ———— I muſt take Poſt immediately : Madam, for ſome few Days I muſt be abſent, and to confirm you, Friend, how much I truſt you, I leave the deareſt Pledge I have on Earth, my Miſtreſs, to your Care

Mill If you lov'd me, you would not take all Occaſions to leave me thus !

Warn [*Aſide*] Do, go to *Kent*, and when you come again, here they are ready for you. [*Shows the Paper.*

Sir Mart What's that you have in your Hand there, Sirrah ?

Warn Pox, what ill Luck was this ! what ſhall I ſay ?

Sir Mart. Sometimes you've Tongue enough, what, are you ſilent ?

Warn 'Tis an Accompt, Sir, of what Money you have loſt ſince you came to Town

Sir Mart I am very glad on't Now I'll make you all ſee the Severity of my Fortune — give me the Paper

Warn Heav'n ! what does he mean to do ? It is not fair writ out, Sir

Sir John Beſides, I am in haſte, another time, Sir ——

Sir Mart Pray, oblige me, Sir —— 'tis but one Minute All People love to be pity'd in their Misfortunes, and ſo do I Will you produce it, Sirrah ?

Warn Dear Maſter !

Sir Mart. Dear Raſcal ! am I Maſter or you ? you Rogue !

Warn Hold yet, Sir, and let me read it . —— you cannot read my Hand.

Sir Mart This is ever his way to be diſparaging me —— but I'll let you ſee, Sirrah, that I can read your Hand better than you your ſelf can

Warn You'll repent it, there's a Trick in't, Sir ——

Sir Mart Is there ſo, Sirrah ? but I'll bring you out of all your Tricks with a Vengeance to you —— [*Reads*] How now ! What's this ? A true Particular of the Eſtate of *Sir John Swallow*, Knight, lying and ſituate in, *&c.*

Sir John This is the very Paper I had loſt . I'm very glad on't, [*Takes the Paper*] it has ſav'd me a moſt unwelcome Journey —— but I will not thank you for the

Cour-

Courtefy, which now I find you never did intend me—
this is Confederacy, I smoke it now —— Come, Madam, let me wait on you to your Father.

Mill. Well, of a witty Man, this was the foolisheft Part
that ever I beheld. [*Exeunt Sir* John, Millifent, *and* Rofe.

Sir Mart I am a Fool, I muft confefs it, and I am
the moft miferable one without thy Help —— but yet it
was fuch a Miftake as any Man might have made.

Warn No doubt on't

Sir Mart Pr'ythee chide me ! this Indifference of
thine wounds me to the Heart

Warn I care not

Sir Mart Wilt thou not help me for this once ?

Warn Sir, I kifs your Hands, I have other Bufinefs.

Sir Mart Dear *Warner* !

Warn. I am inflexible

Sir Mart Then I am refolv'd I'll kill my felf

Warn. You are Mafter of your own Body

Sir Mart Will you let me damn my Soul ?

Warn. At your Pleafure, as the Devil and you can
agree about it

Sir Mart D'ye fee, the Point's ready ? Will you do
nothing to fave my Life ?

Warn Not in the leaft

Sir Mart Farewel, hard-hearted *Warner*

Warn Adieu, foft-headed Sir *Martin*

Sir Mart Is it poffible ?

Warn Why don't you difpatch, Sir ? why all thefe
Preambles ?

Sir Mart. I'll fee thee hang'd firft I know thou
wou'dft have me kill'd, to get my Cloaths.

Warn I knew it was but a Copy of your Countenance , People in this Age are not fo apt to kill themfelves

Sir Mart Here are yet ten Pieces in my Pocket, take
'em, and let's be Friends

Warn You know the Eafinefs of my Nature, and that
makes you work upon it fo Well, Sir —— for this once
I caft an Eye of Pity on you — but I muft have ten
more in Hand, before I can ftir a Foot.

Sir Mart As I am a true Gamefter, I have loft all but thefe —— but if thou'lt lend me them, I ll give 'em thee again.

Wain I'll rather truft you till to-morrow;
Once more look up, I bid you hope the beft.
Why fhould your Folly make your Love mifcarry,
Since Men firft play the Fools, and then they marry?

[*Exeunt.*

A C T,

ACT IV. SCENE I.

Enter Sir Martin Mar-all *and* Warner.

Sir *Mart* BUT are they to be married this Day in
private, say you?

Warn 'Tis so concluded, Sir, I dare assure you.

Sir *Mart*. But why so soon, and in private?

Warn So soon, to prevent the Designs upon her;
and in private, to save the effusion of Christian Money

Sir *Mart* It strikes to my Heart already, in fine, I
am a dead Man. — *Warner.*

Warn. Well, go your ways, I'll try what may be done
Look if he will stir now; your Rival and the old Man
will see us together, we are just below the Window.

Sir *Mart*. Thou can'st not do't.

Warn On the peril of my twenty Pieces be it.

Sir *Mart*. But I have found a way to help thee out,
trust to my Wit but once.

Warn Name your Wit, or think you have the least
Grain of Wit once more, and I'll lay it down for ever

Sir *Mart* You are a sawcy masterly Companion, and
so I leave you.   [*Exit*

Warn. Help, help, good People, Murther! Murther!
    Enter Sir John *and* Moody

Sir *John* and *Mood* How now, what's the Matter?

Warn I am abus'd, I am beaten, I am lam'd for ever.

Mood. Who has us'd thee so?

Warn The Rogue my Master.

Sir *John*. What was the Offence?

Warn A trifle, just nothing

Sir *John*. That's very strange

Warn It was for telling him he lost too much at Play;
I meant him nothing but well, Heav'n knows, and he in
a cursed damn'd Humour would needs revenge his Losses
                                                    upon

upon me. A'kick'd me, took away my Money, and turn'd me off, but if I take it at his Hands ——

Mood By Cox-nowns, it was an ill natur'd Part, nay, I thought no better would come on't, when I heard him at his Vows to gads, and In fines.

Warn But if I live I'll cry Quittance with him He had engag'd me to get Mrs *Millifent* your Daughter for him but if I do not all that ever I can to make her hate him, a great Booby, an over grown Oaf, a conceited *Bartholomew*——

Sir John Pr'ythee leave off thy Choler, and hear me a little. I have had a great mind to thee a long time, if thou think'ft my Service better than his, from this Minute I entertain thee

Warn With all my Heart, Sir, and fo much the rather, that I may fpight him with it.——This was the moft propitious Fate——

Mood. Propitious! and Fate! what a damn'd Scanderbag Rogue art thou to talk at this rate! hark you, Sirrah, one Word more of this Gibberifh, and I'll fet you packing from your new Service, I'll neither have Propitious nor Fate come within my Doors.——

Sir John. Nay, pray Father.——

Warn Good old Sir be pacify'd, I was pouring out a little of the Dregs that I had left in me of my former Service, and now they are gone, my Stomach's clear of 'em.

Sir John. This Fellow is come in an happy Hour; for now, Sir, you and I may go to prepare the Licence, and in the mean time he may have an Eye upon your Daughter.

Warn If you pleafe I'll wait upon her 'till fhe's ready, and then bring her to what Church you fhall appoint.

Mood But, Friend, you'll find fhe'll hang an Arfe, and be very loth to come along with you, and therefore I had beft ftay behind, and bring her my felf.

Warn. I warrant you I have a Trick for that, Sir. She knows nothing of my being turn'd away, fo I'll come to her as from Sir *Martin*, and under pretence of carrying her to him, conduct her to you.

Sir

Sir John My better Angel ——

Mood. By th' Mefs 'twas well thought on, well Son, go you before, I'll fpeak but one Word for a Difh or two at Dinner, and follow you to the Licence-Office. Sirrah — ftay you here — 'till my return

[*Ex Sir* John *and* Moody

Warn folus Was there ever fuch a lucky Rogue as I! I had always a good Opinion of my Wit, but could never think I had fo much as now I find. I have now gain'd an Opportunity to carry away Miftrefs *Millifent,* for my Mafter to get his Miftrefs by means of his Rival, to receive all his Happinefs, where he could expect nothing but Mifery: After this Exploit I will have *Lilly* draw me in the Habit of a Heroe, with a Lawrel on my Temples, and an Infcription below it. *This is* Warner *the Flower of Serving-men*

Enter *Meffenger.*

Meff. Pray do me the favour to help me to the Speech of Mr. *Moody.*

Warn. What's your Bufinefs?

Meff I have a Letter to deliver to him.

Warn. Here he comes, you may deliver it your felf to him.

Enter Moody.

Meff. Sir, a Gentleman met me at the Corner of the next Street, and bid me give this into your own Hands.

Mood Stay, Friend, 'till I have read it.

Meff. He told me, Sir, it requir'd no Anfwer.

[*Exit Meff*

Mood reads *Sir, permit me, though a Stranger, to give you Counfel, fome young Gallants have had Intelligence, that this Day you intend privately to marry your Daughter, the rich Heirefs; and, in fine, above twenty of them have difperfed themfelves to watch her going out: Therefore put it off, if you will avoid Mifchief, and be advifed by*

Your unknown Servant.

Mood By the Mackings I thought there was no good in't, when I faw *in fine* there; there are fome Papifhes,

I'll

I'll warrant, that lie in wait for my Daughter, or elfe
they are no *Englifhmen*, but fome of your *French* Outa-
lian-Rogues , I owe him Thanks however, this unknown Friend of mine, that told me on't. *Warner*, no
Wedding to Day, *Warner*

Warn Why, what's the Matter, Sir ?

Mood. I fay no more, but fome wifer than fome, I'll
keep my Daughter at home this Afternoon, and a Fig
for all thefe Outalians   [*Exit* Moody.

Warn So, here's another Trick of Fortune as unexpect-
ed for bad, as the other was for good   Nothing vexes
me, but that I had made my Game cock-fure, and then
to be back-gammon'd . It muft needs be the Devil that
writ this Letter, he ow'd my Mafter a fpite, and has
paid him to the purpofe   And here he comes as merry
too, he little thinks what Misfortune has befal'n him,
and for my part I am afham'd to tell him

               Enter Sir Martin *loughing*

     Sir Mart Warner, fuch a Jeft, *Warner* [*Laughs again.*

Warn What a Murrain is the Matter, Sir ? Where
lies this Jeft that tickles you ?

     Sir Mart Let me laugh out my Laugh, and I'll tell
thee   [*Laughs again.*

Warn. I wifh you may have caufe for all this Mirth

     Sir Mart Hereafter, *Warner*, be it known unto thee, I
will endure no more to be thy May-game   Thou fhalt no
more dare to tell me, I fpoil thy Projects, and difcover
thy Defigns ; for I have play'd fuch a Prize, without thy
Help, of my own Mother-wit, ('tis true I am hafty fometimes, and fo do Harm , but when I have a Mind to fhew
my felf, there's no Man in *England*, though I fay't, comes
near me as to point of Imagination) I'll make thee ac
knowledge I have laid a Plot that has a Soul in't

Warn Pray, Sir, keep me no longer in Ignorance of
this rare Invention

     Sir Mart Know then, *Warner*, that when I left thee,
I was poffefs'd with a terrible Fear, that my Miftrefs
fhould be married   Well, thought I to my felf, and
muft'ring up all the Forces of my Wit, I did produce
fuch a Stratagem.

                                   Warn.

Warn But what was it?

Sir Mart I feign'd a Letter as from an unknown Friend to *Moody*, wherein I gave him to underftand, that if his Daughter went out this Afternoon, she would infallibly be snapt by some young Fellows that lay in wait for her

Warn Very good

Sir Mart That which follows is yet better, for he I sent affures me, that in that very nick of time my Letter came, her Father was juft fending her abroad with a very foolifh rafcally Fellow that was with him

Warn And did you perform all this a'god's Name? could you do this wonderful Miracle without giving your Soul to the Devil for his Help?

Sir Mart I tell thee Man I did it, and it was done by the Help of no Devil, but this Familiar of my own Brain, how long would it have been ere thou could'ft have thought of fuch a Project? *Martin* faid to his Man, *Who's the Fool now?*

Warn Who's the Fool? why, who ufes to be the Fool? he that ever was fince I knew him, and ever will be fo!

Sir Mart What a Pox! I think thou art grown envious, not one Word in my Commendation?

Warn Faith, Sir, my Skill is too little to praife you as you deferve; but if you would have it according to my poor Ability, you are one that had a Knock in your Cradle, a conceited Lack-wit, a defigning Afs, a hair-brain'd Fop, a confounded bufy Brain, with an eternal Wind-mill in it, this, in fhort, Sir, is the Contents of your Panegyrick

Sir Mart But what the Devil have I done, to fet you thus againft me?

Warn Only this, Sir, I was the foolifh rafcally Fellow that was with *Moody*, and your Worfhip was he to whom I was to bring his Daughter

Sir Mart But how could I know this? I am no Witch.

Warn No, I'll be fworn for you, you are no Conjurer. Will you go, Sir?

Sir Mart Will you hear my Juftifications?

Warn Shall I fee the Back of you? fpeak not a Word in your Defence   [*Shoves him*

Sir

Sir Mart This is the strangeſt Luck now — [*Exit*

Warn I'm reſolv'd this Devil of his ſhall never weary me, I will overcome him, I will invert ſomething that ſhall ſtand good in ſpite of his Folly   Let me ſee——

Enter Lord

Lord Here he is —— I muſt venture on him, for the Tyranny of this old Lady is unſupportable, ſince I have made her my Confident, there paſſes not an Hour but ſhe paſſes a pull at my Purſe-ſtrings, I ſhall be ruined if I do not quit my ſelf of her ſuddenly   I find now, by ſad Experience, that a Miſtreſs is much more chargeable than a Wife, and after a little time too, grows full as dull and inſignificant — Mr. *Warner* ! have you a mind to do your ſelf a Courteſy, and me another ?

Warn I think, my Lord, the Queſtion need not be much diſputed, for I have always had a great Service for your Lordſhip, and ſome little Kindneſs for my ſelf.

Lord What if you ſhould propoſe Miſtreſs *Chriſtian* as a Wife to your Maſter ? You know he's never like to compaſs t'other.

Warn I cannot tell that, my Lord——

Lord Five Hundred Pounds are yours at the Day of Marriage

Warn Five Hundred Pounds ! 'tis true, the Temptation is very ſweet, and powerful, the Devil, I confeſs, has done his Part, and many a good Murder and Treaſon have been committed at a cheaper rate, but yet —

Lord What yet —

Warn To confeſs the Truth, I am reſolv'd to beſtow my Maſter upon that other Lady (as difficult as your Lordſhip thinks it) for the Honour of my Wit is engag'd in it   Will it not be the ſame to your Lordſhip, were ſhe marry'd to any other ?

Lord The very ſame

Warn Come, my Lord, not to diſſemble with you any longer, I know where it is that your Shoe wrings you I have obſerv'd ſomething in the Houſe, betwixt ſome Parties that ſhall be nameleſs   And know that you have been taking up Linnen at a much dearer rate, than you might have had it at any Draper's in Town

Lord

Lord I fee I have not danc'd in a Net before you.

Warn As for that old Lady, whom Hell confound, fhe is the greateft Jilt in Nature, Cheat is her ftudy, all her Joy to cozen, fhe loves nothing but her felf, and draws all Lines to that corrupted Centre

Lord. I have found her out, though late: Firft, I'll undertake I ne'er enjoy'd her Nieee under the rate of five hundred Pounds a time; never was Woman's Flefh held up fo high Every Night I find out for a new Maiden-head, and fhe has fold it me as often as ever Mother *Temple, Bennet,* or *Gifford,* have put off boil'd Capons for Quails and Partridges

Warn This is nothing to what Bills you'll have when fhe's brought to Bed, after her hard Bargain, as they call it; then cramm'd Capons, Pea-hens, Chickens in the greafe, Pottages, and Fricacies, Wine from *Shailing,* and *La-fronds,* with New-River, clearer by Sixpence the Pound than ever God Almighty made it; then Midwife—Dry Nurfe—Wet Nurfe—and all the reft of their Accomplices, wih Cradle, Baby-Clouts, and Bearing-Cloths—Poffet, Cawdels, Broth, Jellies, and Gravies; and behind all thefe, Glifters, Suppofitors, and a barbarous 'Pothecary's Bill, more inhuman than a Tailor's

Lord. I fweat to think on't.

Warn Well, my Lord! chear up! I have found a way to rid you of it all, within a fhort time you fhall know more; yonder appears a young Lady whom I muft needs fpeak with, pleafe you go in and prepare the old Lady and your Miftrefs

Lord. Good Luck, and five hundred Pounds attend thee.   [*Exit.*

    Enter Millifent *and* Rofe *above*

Mill. I am refolv'd I'll never marry him!

Rofe So far you are right, Madam

Mill. But, how to hinder it, I cannot poffibly tell; For my Father preffes me to it, and will take no denial. Would I knew fome way——

Warn Madam, I'll teach you the very neareft, for I have juft now found it out.

                                      Rofe.

Rose Are you there, Mr Littleplot?

Warn. Studying to deferve thee, *Rose*, by my Diligence for thy Lady; I ftand here, methinks, juft like a wooden *Mercury*, to point her out the way to Matrimony.

Rose Or, Serving-man like, ready to carry up the hot Meat for your Mafter, and then to fall upon the cold your felf.

Warn I know not what you call the cold, but I believe I fhall find warm Work on't. In the firft place then I muft acquaint you, that I have feemingly put off my Mafter, and enter'd my felf into Sir *John*'s Service.

Mill Moft excellent!

Warn. And thereupon, but bafe ——————

Enter Moody

Mill Something he would tell us, but fee what Luck's here!

Mood. How now, Sirrah? Are you fo great there already?

Mill. I find my Father's jealous of him ftill!

Warn. Sir, I was only teaching my young Lady a new Song, and if you pleafe you fhall hear it

S I N G S.

Make ready, fair Lady, to Night,
And ftand at the Door below,
For I will be there
To receive you with Care,
And to your true Love you fhall go.

Mood. Ods bobs, this is very pretty.

Mill Ay, fo is the Lady's Anfwer too, if I could but hit on't.

S I N G S.

And when the Stars twinkle fo bright,
Then down to the Door will I creep,
To my Love will I fly,
E'er the Jealous can fpy,
And leave my old Daddy afleep.

Mood Bodikins, I like not that so well, to cozen her old Father, it may be my own Case another time

Rose Oh Madam! yonder's your Persecutor return'd

Enter Sir John.

Mill I'll into my Chamber to avoid the sight of him as long as I can, Lord! that my old doating Father should throw me away upon such an *Ignoramus,* and deny me to such a Wit as Sir *Martin*

[*Exeunt* Mill *and* Rose *from above.*

Mood O Son! here has been the most villainous Tragedy against you.

Sir John What Tragedy? Has there been any Blood shed since I went?

Mood No Blood shed, but, as I told you, a most damnable Tragedy

Warn A Tragedy! I'll be hang'd if he does not mean a Stratagem

Mood. Jack Sawce! if I say it is a Tragedy, it shall be a Tragedy in spite of you, teach your Grandam how to piss — what — I hope I am old enough to spout *English* with you, Sir.

Sir John But what was the Reason you came not after me?

Mood 'Twas well I did not, I'll promise you, there were those would have made bold with Mistress Bride; an' if she had stirr'd out of Doors, there were Whipsters abroad i'faith, Padders of Maiden-heads, that would have truss'd her up, and pick'd the Lock of her Affections, ere a Man could have said, what's this But by good Luck I had warning of it by a Friend's Letter

Sir John The Remedy for all such Dangers is easy, you may send for a Parson, and have the Business dispatch'd at home

Mood. A Match, i'faith, do you provide a *Domine,* and I'll go tell her our Resolutions, and hearten her up against the day of Battel [*Exit*

Sir John Now I think on't, this Letter must needs come from Sir *Martin,* a Plot of his, upon my Life, to hinder our Marriage.

Warn.

Warn. I see, Sir, you'll still mistake him for a Wit; but I am much deceiv'd, if that Letter came not from another hand.

Sir John From whom, I pr'ythee?

Warn Nay, for that you shall excuse me, Sir, I do not love to make a Breach betwixt Persons that are to be so near related.

Sir John Thou seem'st to imply that my Mistress was in the Plot

Warn Can you make a Doubt on't? Do you not know she ever lov'd him, and can you hope she has so soon forsaken him? You may make your self miserable, if you please, by such a Marriage

Sir John When she is once mine, her Virtue will secure me

Warn Her Virtue!

Sir John What, do you make a mock on't?

Warn Not I, I assure you, Sir, I think it no such jesting Matter

Sir John Why, is she not honest?

Warn Yes, in my Conscience is she, for Sir Martin's Tongue's no Slander

Sir John But does he say to the contrary?

Warn If one would believe him, which for my Part I do not, he has in a manner confess'd it to me

Sir John Hell and Damnation!

Warn Courage, Sir, never vex your self, I'll warrant you 'tis all a Lie

Sir John But, how shall I be sure 'tis so?

Warn When you are married you'll soon make trial, whether she be a Maid or no

Sir John I do not love to make that Experiment at my own Cost.

Warn Then you must never marry

Sir John Ay, but they have so many Tricks to cheat a Man, which are entail'd from Mother to Daughter through all Generations, there's no keeping a Lock for that Door, for which every one has a Key

Warn As for Example, then drawing up their Breaths with Oh! you hurt me, can you be so cruel? then the

G 2

next

next Day ſhe ſteals a Viſit to her Lover, that did you the Courteſy before-hand, and in private tells him how ſhe cozened you; twenty to one but ſhe takes out another Leſſon with him to practiſe the next Night

Sir John All this while miſerable I muſt be their May-game.

Warn 'Tis well, if you eſcape ſo; for commonly he ſtrikes in with you, and becomes your Friend.

Sir John Deliver me from ſuch a Friend, that ſtays behind with my Wife, when I gird on my Sword to go abroad.

Warn. Ay, there's your Man, Sir, beſides he will be ſure to watch your Haunts, and tell her of them, that if occaſion be, ſhe may have where-withal to recriminate: At leaſt ſhe will ſeem to be jealous of you, and who would ſuſpect a jealous Wife?

Sir John. All manner of ways I am moſt miſerable.

Warn But, if ſhe be not a Maid when you marry her, ſhe may make a good Wife afterwards, 'tis but imagining you have taken ſuch a Man's Widow.

Sir John If that were all; but the Man will come and claim her again

Warn Examples have been frequent of thoſe that have been wanton, and yet afterwards take up

Sir John Ay, the ſame thing they took up before

Warn The Truth is, an honeſt ſimple Girl that's Ignorant of all things, maketh the beſt Matrimony· There is ſuch Pleaſure in inſtructing her; the beſt is, there's not one Dunce in all the Sex, ſuch a one with a good Fortune———

Sir John Ay, but where is ſhe, *Warner?*

Warn Near enough, but that you are too far engag'd

Sir John Engag'd to one that hath given me the Earreſt of Cuckoldom before-hand?

Warn What think you then of Mrs. *Chriſtian* here in the Houſe? There's five thouſand Pounds and a better Penny.

Sir John. Ay, but is ſhe Fool enough?

Warn. She's none of the wiſe Virgins, I can aſſure you.

Sir

Sir John Dear *Warner*, ftep into the next Room, and inviegle her out this way, that I may fpeak to her.

Warn Remember above all things, you keep this Wooing fecret, if it takes the leaft Wind, old *Moody* will be fure to hinder it.

Sir John. Do'ft thou think I fhall get her Aunt's Confent ?

Warn Leave that to me   [*Exit* Warn.

Sir John. How happy a Man fhall I be, if I can but compafs this ! and what a Precipice have I avoided ! then the Revenge too is fo fweet to fteal a Wife under her Father's Nofe, and leave 'em in the Lurch who have abus'd me, well, fuch a Servant as this *Warner* is a Jewel.

Enter Warner *and Mrs* Chriftian *to him.*

Warn. Tnere fhe is, Sir, now I'll go to prepare her Aunt.   [*Exit.*

Sir John Sweet Miftrefs, I am come to wait upon you.

Chr Truly you are too good to wait on me

Sir John. And in the Condition of a Suitor.

Chr As how, forfooth ?

Sir John. To be fo happy as to marry you.

Chr. O Lord, I would not marry for any thing !

Sir John. Why ? 'tis the honeft End of Woman-kind

Chr. Twenty Years hence, forfooth. I would not lye in Bed with a Man for a World, their Beards will fo prickle one.

Sir John. Pah —— What an innocent Girl it is, and very Child ! I like a Colt that never yet was back'd; for fo I fhall make her what I lift, and mould her as I will ; Lord ! her Innocency makes me laugh my Cheeks all wet —— Sweet Lady ——   [*Afide.*

Chr I'm but a Gentlewoman, forfooth.

Sir John Well then, fweet Miftrefs, if I get your Friends Confent, fhall I have yours?

Chr. My old Lady may do what fhe will, forfooth, but by my truly, I hope fhe will have more care of me, than to marry me yet, Lord blefs me, what fhould I do with a Husband ?

Sir John Well, Sweet-heart, then inftead of wooing ꝛo, I muft wooe my old Lady

Chr.

Chr. Indeed, Gentleman, my old Lady is married already. Cry you mercy, forſooth, I think you are a Knight

Sir John Happy in that Title only to make you Lady.

Chr. Believe me, Mr Knight, I would not be a Lady, it makes Folks proud, and ſo humourous, and ſo ill Huſwiſes, forſooth.

Sir John. Pah ———— ſhe's a Baby, the ſimpleſt thing that ever yet I knew; the happieſt Man I ſhall be in the World; for ſhould I have my Wiſh, it ſhould be to keep School, and teach the bigger Girls, and here in one my Wiſh it is abſolv'd

Enter Lady Dupe.

L. Dupe. By your, leave, Sir, I hope this noble Knight will make you happy, and you make him ————

Chr. What ſhould I make him?   [*Sighing.*

L Dupe Marry, you ſhall make him happy in a good Wife

Chr I will not marry, Madam

L Dupe You Fool!

Sir John Pray, Madam, let me ſpeak with you, on my Soul 'tis the pretty ſt Innocent'ſt thing in the World.

L Dupe Indeed, Sir, ſhe knows little beſides her Work, and her Prayers; but I'll talk with the Fool.

Sir John. Deal gently with her, dear Madam

L Dupe Come, *Chriſtian*, will not you marry this noble Knight?

Chr Yes, yes, yes ————   [*Sobbingly.*

L Dupe Sir, it ſhall be to Night

Sir John This Innocence is a Dowry beyond all price.
            [*Exeunt old Lady, and Mrs* Chriſtian.

Enter Sir Martin, *to Sir* John *muſing*

Sir Mart You are very melancholy methinks, Sir.

Sir John You are miſtaken, Sir

Sir Mart You may diſſemble as you pleaſe, but Mrs. *Milliſent* lyes at the Bottom of your Heart

Sr John My Heart, I aſſure you, has no room for ſo poor a Trifle

Sir Mart Sure you think to wheedle me, would you have me imagine you do not Love her?

Sir John.

Sir John. Love her! why should you think me such a Sot? love a Proftitute an infamous Perfon!

Sir Mart Fair and foft, good Sir John

Sir John You fee I am no very obftrate Rival, I leave the Field free to you Go on, Sir, and purfue your good Fortune, and be as happy as fuch a Common Creature can make thee

Sir Mart. This is *Hebrew-Greek* to me, but I muft tell you, Sir, I will not fuffer my Divinity to be prophan'd by fuch a Tongue as yours

Sir John Believe it, whate'er I fay, I can quote my Author for

Sir Mart Then, Sir, whoever told it you, ly'd in his Throat, d'you fee, and deeper than that, d'ye fee, in his Stomach, and his Guts d'ye fee· Tell me fhe's a common Perfon! he's a Son of a Whore that faid it, and I'll make him eat his Words, though he fpoke 'em in a Privy-houfe

Sir John What if *Warner* told me fo? I hope you'll grant him to be a competent Judge in fuch a Bufinefs

Sir Mart Did that precious Rafcal fay it? ——Now I think on't, I'll not believe you In fine, Sir, I'll hold you an even Wager he denies it

Sir John. I'll lay you ten to one, he juftifies it to your Face

Sir Mart I'll make him give up the Ghoft under my Fift, if he does not deny it

Sir John I'll cut off his Ears upon the Spot, if he does not ftand to't

Enter Warner

Sir Mart. Here he comes in Pudding-time to refolve the Queftion: Come hither, you lying Varlet, hold up your Hand at the Bar of Juftice, and anfwer me to what I fhall demand.

Warn What a Goodier is the matter, Sir?

Sir Mart Thou Spawn of the old Serpent, fruitful in nothing but in Lies!

Warn. A very fair Beginning this

Sir Mart. Didft thou dare to caft thy Venom upon fuch a Saint as Mrs. *Millifent,* to traduce her Virtue, and fay it was adulterate?

G 4 *Warn.*

Warn. Not guilty, my Lord.

Sir *Mart* I told you so

Sir *John* How, Mr Rafcal! have you forgot what you faid but now concerning Sir *Martin* and Mrs *Milli-fent?* I'll ftop the Lie down your Throat, if you dare deny't

Sir *Mart* Say you fo' are you there again i'faith?

Warn Pray pacify your felf, Sir, 'twas a Plot of my own devifing

Sir *Mart* Leave off your winking and your pinking, with a Horfe-pox t'ye, I'll underftand none of it; tell me in plain *Englifh* the truth of the Bufinefs: For an you were my own Brother, you fhould pay for it Belie my Miftrefs! what a Pox d'ye think I have no fenfe of Honour?

Warn. What the Devil's the matter w'ye? Either be at quiet, or I'll refolve to take my Heels, and be gone.

Sir *Mart.* Stop Thief there' what, did you think to 'fcape the Hand of Juftice? [*Lays hold on him*] The beft on't is, Sirrah, your Heels are not altogether fo nimble as your Tongue   [*Beats him.*

Warn. Help' Murder! Murder!

Sir *Mart* Confefs, you Rogue, then.

Warn. Hold your Hands, I think the Devil's in you,— I tell you 'tis a Device of mine.

Sir *Mart.* And have you no Body to devife it on but my Miftrefs, the very Map of Innocence?

Sir *John* Moderate your Anger, good Sir *Martin.*

Sir *Mart.* By your Patience, Sir, I'll chaftife him a-bundantly

Sir *John* That's a little too much, Sir, by your Favour, to beat him in my Prefence

Sir *Mart.* That's a good one i'faith, your Prefence fhall hinder me from beating my own Servant

Warn O Traytor to all Senfe and Reafon! he's going to difcover that too

Sir *Mart.* An I had a mind to beat him to Mummy, he's my own, I hope

Sir *John* At prefent, I muft tell you, he's mine, Sir.

Sir *Mart* Hey-day! here's fine juggling'

Warn.

Warn Stop yet, Sir, you are juft upon the Brink of a Precipice

Sir Mart. What is't thou mean'ft now ?——— ah Lord ! my Mind mif-gives me I have done fome Fault, b it would I were hang'd if I can find it out   [*fide*

Warn. There's no making him underftand me

Sir Mart. Pox on't, come what will, I'll not be fac'd down with a Lie; I fay he is my Man.

Sir John Pray remember your felf better; did not you turn him away for fome Fault lately, and laid a Livery of black and blue on his Back before he went ?

Sir Mart The Devil of any Fault, or any black and blue that I remember. Either the Rafcal put fome Trick upon you, or you would upon me.

Sir John O-ho, then it feems the cudgelling and turning away were pure Invention ; I am glad I underftand it

Sir Mart. In fine, it's all fo damn'd a Lie———

Warn Alas! he has forgot it, Sir; good Wits, you know, have bad Memories

Sir John No, no, Sir, that fhall not ferve your Turn, you may return when you pleafe to your old Mafter, I give you a fair Difcharge, and a glad Man I am to be fo rid of you. Were you thereabouts i'faith? What a Snake I had entertain'd into my Bofom? Fare you well. Sir, and lay your next Plot better between you, I advife you.   [*Exit Sir* John

Warn Lord, Sir, how you ftand ! as you were nip'd i'th' head Have you done any new Piece of Folly, that makes you look fo like an Afs ?

Sir Mart Here's three pieces of Gold yet, if I had the Heart to offer it thee. [*Holds the Gold afar off trembling.*

Warn. Noble Sir, what have I done to deferve fo great a Liberality ? I confefs if you had beaten me for my own Fault, if you had utterly deftroyed all my Projects, then it might ha' been expected that ten or twenty Pieces fhould have been offer'd by way of Recompence or Satisfaction.———

SIR *Mart.* Nay, an you be so full o'your Flouts, your Friend and Servant; who the Devil could tell the Meaning of your Signs and Tokens, an you go to that?

Warn. You are no Ass then?

SIR *Mart* Well, Sir, to do you Service, d'ye see, I am an Ass in a fair way; will that satisfie you?

Warn For this once produce those three Pieces, I am contented to receive that inconsiderable Tribute, or make 'em six, and I'll take the Fault upon my self.

SIR *Mart.* Are we Friends then? If we are, let me advise you——

Warn Yet advising——

SIR *Mart.* For no harm, good *Warner*; But pray next time make me of your Council, let me enter into the Business, instruct me in every Point, and then if I discover all, I am resolv'd to give over Affairs, and retire from the World

Warn Agreed, it shall be so; but let us now take breath a while, then on again

For though we had the worst, those Heats are past,

We'll whip and spur, and fetch him up at last. [*Exeunt*

ACT

ACT V. SCENE I.

Enter Lord, Lady Dupe, *Miſtreſs* Chriſtian, Roſe, *and* Warner

Lord YOUR Promiſe is admirably made good to me, that Sir *John Swallow* ſhould be this Night married to Mis *Chriſtian,* inſtead of that, he is more deeply engag'd than ever with old *Moody*

Warn. I cannot help thoſe ebbs and flows of Fortune.

L *Dupe* I am ſure my Niece ſuffers moſt in't, he's come off to her with a cold Compliment of a miſtake in his Miſtreſs's Virtue, which he has now found out, by your Maſter's Folly, to be a Plot of yours to ſeparate them.

Chr To be forſaken when a Woman has given her Conſent!

Lord 'Tis the ſame Scorn, as to have a Town render'd up, and afterwards ſlighted

Roſe You are a ſweet Youth, Sir, to uſe my Lady ſo, when ſhe depended on you, is this the Faith of a *Valet de Chambre?* I would be aſham'd to be ſuch a diſhonour to my Profeſſion, it will reflect upon us in time, we ſhall be ruin'd by your good Example

Warn As how, my dear Lady Embaſſadreſs?

Roſe Why, they ſay the Women govern their Ladies, and you govern us So if you play faſt and looſe, not a Gallant will bribe us for our Good-wills; the gentle *Guinea* will now go to the Ordinary, which us'd as duly to ſteal into our Hands at the Stair-foot, as into Mr. Doctor's at parting.

Lord.

Lord. Night's come, and I expect your Promise.

L. *Dupe* Fail with me if you think good, Sir.

Chr I give no more Time

Rose And if my Miftress go to Bed a Maid to Night———

Warn. Hey-day! you are dealing with me, as they do with the Bankrupts, call in all your Debts together; there's no poffibility of Payment at this rate, but I'll coin for you all as faft as I can, I affure you

L *Dupe* But you muft not think to pay us with falfe Mony, as you have done hitherto

Rose Leave off your Mountebank Tricks with us, and fall to your Bufinefs in good Earneft.

Warn Faith, and I will *Rose*; for to confefs the Truth, I am a kind of a Mountebank, I have but one Cure for all your Difeafes, that is, that my Mafter may marry Mrs *Millifent*, for then Sir *John Swallow* will of himfelf return to Mrs *Chriftian*

Lord He fays true, and therefore we muft be all helping to that defign

Warn. I'll put you upon fomething, give me but a thinking time. In the firft Place, get a Warrant and Bailiffs to arreft Sir *John Swallow* upon a Promife of Marriage to Mrs *Chriftian*

Lord Very good

L *Dupe* We'll all fwear it.

Warn I never doubted your Ladyfhip in the leaft, Madam——— for the reft we will confider here-after.

Lord Leave this to us.

       [*Ex Lord,* L Dupe. Mill *and* Chr.

Warn *Rose*, where's thy Lady?

Mill [*above.*] What have you to fay to her?

Warn Only to tell you, Madam, I am going forward in the great Work of Projection

Mill I know not whether you will deferve my Thanks when the Work's done.

Warn Madam, I hope you are not become indifferent to my Mafter?

                            Mill.

Mill If he fhould prove a Fool after all your crying up his Wit, I fhall be a miferable Woman

Warn A Fool! that were a good Jeſt i'faith but how comes your Ladyſhip to fuſpect it?

Roſe. I have heard, Madam, your greateſt Wits have ever a Touch of Madneſs and Extravagance in them, ſo perhaps has he

Warn. There's nothing more diſtant than Wit and Folly, yet like Eaſt and Weſt, they may meet in a Point, and produce Actions that are but a Hair's breadth from one another.

Roſe I'll undertake he has Wit enough to make one laugh at him a whole Day together. He's a moſt Comical Perſon

Mill For all this I will not ſwear he is no Fool; he has ſtill diſcovered all your Plots.

Warn. O Madam, that's the common Fate of your Machivilians, they draw their Deſigns ſo ſubtile, that their very Fineneſs breaks them.

Mill However, I'm reſolv'd to be on the ſure ſide, I will have certain proof of his Wit, before I marry him.

Warn Madam, I'll give you one, he wears his Cloaths like a great Sloven, and that's a ſure ſign of Wit, he neglects his outward Parts, beſides, he ſpeaks *French,* ſings, dances, plays upon the Lute

Mill Does he do all this, ſay you?

Warn Moſt divinely, Madam

Mill I ask no more, then let him give me a Serenade immediately; but let him ſtand in the View, I'll not be cheated.

Warn He ſhall do't Madam · ——— But how, the Devil knows; for he ſings like a Scritch-Owl, and never touch'd the Lute   [*Aſide.*

Mill You'll ſee't perform'd?

Warn Now I think on't, Madam, this will but retard our Enterprife.

Mill Either let him do't, or ſee me no more

Warn Well, it ſhall be done, Madam, but where's your Father? will not he over-hear it?

Mill.

Mill As good hap is, he's below Stairs, talking with a Seaman, that has brought him News from the *East-Indies*

Warn What Concernment can he have there ?

Mill. He had a Baftard-Son there, whom he loved extreamly but not having any News from him thefe many Years, concluded him dead ; this Son he expects within thefe three Days

Warn When did he fee him laft ?

Mill Not fince he was feven Years old

Warn A fudden thought comes into my Head to make him appear before his Time , let my Mafter pafs for him, and by that means he may come into the Houfe unfufpected by her Father, or his Rival.

Mill According as he performs his Serenade, I'll talk with you———— make hafte———— I muft retire a little.   [*Exit* Mill *from above*

Rofe I'll inftruct him moft rarely, he fhall never be found out; but in the mean time, what wilt thou do for a Serenade ?

Warn Faith, I am a little non-plus'd on the fudden, but a warm Confolation from thy Lips, *Rofe*, would fet my Wits a working again.

Rofe Adieu, *Warner*   [*Exit*

Warn Inhuman *Rofe*, adieu ———— Blockhead *Warner*, into what a Premunire haft thou brought thy felf, this 'tis to be fo forward to promife for another ——— but to be Godfather to a Fool, to promife and vow he fhould do any thing like a Chriftian ————

Enter Sir Martin Mar-all

Sir *Mart.* Why, how now Bully, in a brown Study ? For my good I warrant it ; there's five Shillings for thee, what, we muft encourage good Wits fometimes

Warn Hang your white Pelf Sure, Sir, by your Largefs you miftake me for *Martin Parker*, the Ballad-maker; your Covetoufnefs has offended my Mufe, and quite dull'd her.

Sir

Sir Mart. How angry the poor Devil is ! In fine, thou art as cholerick as a Cook by a Fire-side

Warn. I am over-heated, like a Gun, with continual discharging my Wit . 'Slife, Sir, I have rarifi'd my Brains for you, 'till they are evaporated, but, come, Sir, do something for your self like a Man, I have engag'd you shall give to your Mistress a Serenade in your proper Person . I'll borrow a Lute for you,

Sir Mart I'll warrant thee I'll do't, Man

Warn. You never learn'd, I do not think you know one Stop

Sir Mart. 'Tis no matter for that, Sir, I'll play as fast as I can, and never stop at all

Warn. Go to, you are an invincible Fool, I see, get up into your Window, and set two Candles by you, take my Landlord's Lute in your Hand, and fumble on't, and make Grimaces with your Mouth, as if you sung; in the mean time, I'll play in the next Room in the dark, and consequently your Mistress, who will come to her Balcony over against you, will think it to be you, and at the end of every Tune, I'll ring the Bell that hangs between your Chamber and mine, that you may know when we have done.

Sir Mart Why, this is fair Play now, to tell a Man before-hand what he must do, Gramercy i'faith, Boy, now if I fail thee ——

Warn About your Business then, your Mistress and her Maid appear already; I'll give you the Sign with the Bell when I am prepar'd, for my Lute is at hand in the Barber's Shop   [*Exeunt.*

Enter Mrs. Millisent, *and* Rose, *with a Candle by 'em above.*

Rose. We shall have rare Musick.

Mill. I wish it prove so; for I suspect the Knight can neither play nor sing

Rose. But if he does, you're bound to pay the Musick, Madam.

Mill.

Mill I'll not believe it, except both my Ears and Eyes are Witnesses.

Rose. But 'tis Night, Madam, and you cannot see 'em; yet he may play admirably in the dark.

Mill. Where's my Father?

Rose. You need not fear him, he's still employ'd with the same Sea-man, and I have set Mrs. *Christian* to watch their Discourse, that betwixt her and me *Warner* may have wherewithal to instruct his Master

Mill. But yet there's fear my Father will find out the Plot.

Rose. Not in the least, for my old Lady has provided two rare Disguises for the Master and the Man

Mill Peace, I hear them beginning to tune the Lute

Rose. And see, Madam, where your true Knight Sir *Martin* is plac'd yonder like *Apollo*, with his Lute in his Hand and his Rays about his Head

> [*Sir* Martin *appears at the adverse Window, a*
> *Tune play'd, when it is done,* Warner *rings,*
> *and Sir* Martin *holds.*

Did he not play most excellently, Madam?

Mill He play'd well, and yet methinks he held his Lute but untowardly

Rose. Dear Madam, peace; now for the Song.

The SONG.

BLIND *Love to this Hour*
Had never like me, a Slave under his Power.
 Then blest be the Dart
 That he threw at my Heart,
  For nothing can prove
A Joy so great as to be wounded with Love.

 My Days, and my Nights,
Are fill'd to the Purpose with Sorrows and Frights;
 From my Heart still I sigh,
 And my Eyes are ne'er dry,
  So that, Cupid *be prais'd,*
I am to the top of Love's Happiness rais'd.

My

My Soul's all on fire,
So that I have the Pleasure to doat and desire;
    Such a pretty soft Pain,
    That it tickles each Vein,
        'Tis the Dream of a Smart,
Which makes me breathe short, when it beats at my Heart.

        Sometimes in a Pet,
When I am despis'd, I my Freedom would get,
    But streight a sweet Smile
    Does my Anger beguile,
        And my Heart does recal,
Then the more I do struggle, the lower I fall.

        Heav'n does not impart
Such a Grace as to love unto ev'ry one's Heart;
    For many may wish
    To be wounded, and miss:
        Then bless be Love's Fire,
And more bless her Eyes that first taught me Desire.

The Song being done, Warner rings again; but Sir Martin
    continues fumbling, and gazing on his Mistress.

Mill. A pretty humour'd Song —— but stay, methinks he plays and sings still, and yet we cannot hear
him —— Play louder, Sir *Martin,* that we may have
the Fruits on't.

Warn [*Peeping*] Death! this abominable Fool will
spoil all again. Damn him, he stands making his Grimaces yonder, and he looks so earnestly upon his Mistress, that he hears me not   [*Rings again.*

Mill. Ah, ah! have I found you out, Sir? now as I
live and breathe, this' is pleasant, *Rose,* —— his Man play'd
and sung for him, and he, it seems, did not know when
he should give over   [Mill. *and* Rose *laugh.*

Warn. They have found him out, and laugh yonder,
as if they would split their Sides. Why Mr. Fool, Oaf,
Coxcomb, will you hear none of your Names?

                                                        Mill

Mill Sir *Martin*, Sir *Martin*, take your Man's Counsel, and keep Time with your Musick

Sir *Mart* [*Peeping*] Hah! what do you say, Madam? how does your Ladyship like my Musick?

Mill O most heav'nly! just like the Harmony of the Spheres, that is to be admired, and never heard

Warn You have ruin'd all by your not leaving off in time

Sir *Mart* What the Devil wou'd you have a Man do, when my Hand is in' well, o' my Conscience I think there is a Fate upon me   [*Noise within*

Mill Look, *Rose*, what's the matter

Rose. 'Tis Sir *John Swallow* pursu'd by the Bailiffs, Madam, according to our Plot, it seems they have dogg d him thus late to his Lodging

Mill That's well! for though I begin not to love this Fool, yet I am glad I shall be rid of him
                    [*Exeunt* Mill *and* Rose.

Enter Sir John *pursued by three Bailiffs over the Stage*

Sir *Mart.* Now I'll redeem all again, my Mistress shall see my Valour, I'm resolv'd on't. Villains, Rogues, Poultroons! what? three upon one? in fine, I'll be with you immediately.   [*Exit.*

Warn. Why, Sir, are you stark mad? have you no Grain of Sense left? He's gone! now is he as earnest in the Quarrel as *Cokes* among the Puppets; 'tis to no purpose whatever I do for him.   [*Exit* Warn

Enter Sir John *and* Sir Martin, *(having driven away the Bailiffs)* Sir Martin *flourisheth his Sword*

Sir *Mart* *Victoria! Victoria!* what Heart, Sir *John*, you have received no harm, I hope?

Sir *John* Not the least, I thank you, Sir, for your timely Assistance, which I will requite with any thing, but the resigning of my Mistress —— Dear Sir *Martin*, a good Night.

                    Sir

Sir Mart. Pray let me wait upon you in, Sir *John.*

Sir John I can find my way to Mrs *Millifent* without you, Sir, I thank you

Sir Mart But pray, what were you to be arrested for?

Sir John I know no more than you, fome little Debts perhaps I left unpaid by my Negligence Once more good Night, Sir 　　　　　　　　　[*Exit*

Sir Mart He's an ungrateful Fellow, and fo, in fine, I fhall tell him when I fee him next ——————— Monfieur ——————

Enter Warner.

Warner, à propos! I hope you'll applaud me now, I have defeated the Enemy, and that in fight of my Miftrefs; Boy, I have charm'd her i'faith with my Valour.

Warn Ay, juft as much as you did e'en now with your Mufick; go, you are fo beaftly a Fool, that a chiding is thrown away upon you.

Sir Mart. Fool in your Face, Sir; call a Man of Honour Fool, when I have juft atchieved fuch an Enterprize —— Gad, now my Blood's up, I am a dangerous Perfon, I can tell you that, *Warner*

Warn Poor Animal, I pity thee!

Sir Mart I grant I am no Mufician, but you muft allow me for a Sword-man, I have beat 'em bravely; and, in fine, I am come off unhurt, fave only a little Scratch i' th' Head

Warn That's impoffible, thou haft a Scull fo thick, no Sword can pierce it; but much good may't d'ye, Sir, with the Fruits of your Valour You refcu'd your Rival, when he was to be arrested, on purpofe to take him off from your Miftrefs

Sir Mart. Why, this is ever the Fate of ingenious Men, nothing thrives they take in Hand.

Enter

Enter Rose

Rose. Sir *Martin*, you have done your ꞇ   ᵗʰ
my Lady, she'll never look upon you more   ,
she's so well satisfied of your Wit and Cou: ɡe, .. a. ᵗhe
will not put you to any further Tryal

Sir *Mart.* Warner, is there no Hopes, *Warner?*

Warn None that I know.

Sir *Mart.* Let's have but one civil Plot more before
we part.

Warn 'Tis to no purpose

Rose. Yet, if he had some golden Friends that would
engage for him the next time ——

Sir *Mart* Here's a *Jacobus* and a *Carolus* will enter
into Bonds for me.

Rose. I'll take their Royal Words for once.

               [*She fetches two Disguises.*

Warn. The Meaning of this, dear *Rose?*

Rose 'Tis in pursuance of thy own Invention, *Warner?* a Child which thy Wit hath begot upon me: But
let us lose no Time. Help! help! dress thy Master, that
he may be *Anthony*, old *Moody*'s Bastard, and thou his,
come from the *East-Indies.*

Sir *Mart* Hey-tarock it ——— now we shall have
Rose's device too, I long to be at it, pray let's hear more
on't?

Rose. Old *Moody* you must know in his younger Years,
when he was a *Cambridge* Scholar, made bold with a
Towns-man's Daughter there, by whom he had a Bastard,
Whose Name was *Anthony*, whom you, Sir *Martin*,
are to represent.

Sir *Mart* I warrant you, let me alone for *Tony*: But
pray go on, *Rose.*

Rose. This Child, in his Father's Time, he durst not
own, but bred him privately in the Isle of *Ely*, 'till he
was seven Years old, and from thence sent him with one
Bonaventure, a Merchant, for the *East-Indies*

Warn. But will not this over-burden your Memory,
Sir?

Sir Mart There's no anſwering thee any thing, thou think'ſt I am good for nothing

Roſe. *Bonaventure* dy'd at *Surat* within two Years, and this *Anthony* has liv'd up and down in the *Mogul's* Country unheard of by his Father 'till this Night, and is expected within theſe three Days : Now if you can paſs for him, you may have admittance into the Houſe, and make an end of all the Buſineſs before the other *Anthony* arrives

Warn But hold, *Roſe*, there's one conſiderable Point omitted ; what was his Mother's Name ?

Roſe. That indeed I had forgot , her Name was *Dorothy*, Daughter to one *Draw-water*, a Vintner at the *Roſe*

Warn. Come, Sir, are you perfect in your Leſſon ? *Anthony Moody*, born in *Cambridge*, bred in the Iſle of *Ely*, ſent into the *Mogul's* Country at ſeven Years old, with one *Bonaventure* a Merchant, who dy'd within two Years, your Mother's Name *Dorothy Draw-water*, the Vintner's Daughter at the *Roſe*

Sir Mart. I have it all *ad unguem*—what do'ſt think I'm a Sot ? But ſtay a little, how have I liv'd all this while in that ſame Country ?

Warn What Country ?——— Pox, he has forgot, already———

Roſe The *Mogul's* Country

Sir Mart Ay, ay, the *Mogul's* Country ! what the Devil, any Man may miſtake a little, but now I have it perfect · But what have I been doing all this while in the *Mogul's* Country ? He's a heathen Rogue, I am afraid I ſhall never hit upon his Name

Warn Why, you have been paſſing your Time there no matter how

Roſe Well, if this paſſes upon the old Man, I'll bring your Buſineſs about again with my Miſtreſs, never fear it, ſtay you here at the Door, I'll go tell the old Man of your Arrival

Warn Well, Sir, now play your Part exactly, and I'll forgive all your former Errors. ———

Sir

Sir Mart. Hang'em, they were only flips of Youth —
how peremptory and domineering this Rogue is ' now
he fees I have need of his Service Would I were out
of his Power again, I would make him lie at my Feet
like any Spaniel.

Enter Moody, *Sir* John, *Lord*, *Lady* Dupe, Millifent,
Chriftian, *and* Rofe

Mood Is he here already, fay'ft thou ? which is he ?
Rofe That Sun-burn'd Gentleman
Mood My dear Boy *Anthony*, do I fee thee again
before I die ? Welcome, welcome
Sir Mart My dear Farher, I know it is you by In-
ftinct ; for methinks I am as like you as if I were fpit
out of your Mouth
Rofe Keep it up, I befeech your Lordfhip
                                    [*Afide to the Lord*
Lord He's wond'rous like indeed.
L Dupe The very Image of him
Mood *Anthony*, You muft falute all this Company
This is my Lord *Dartmouth*, this my Lady *Dupe*, this
her Niece Mrs *Chriftian*   [*He falutes them*
Sir Mart And that's my Sifter, methinks I have a
good Refemblance of her too Honeft Sifter, I muft
needs kifs you, Sifter
Warn This Fool will difcover himfelf, I forefee it
already by his Carriage to her.
Mood And now *Anthony*, pray tell us a little of your
Travels
Sir Mart Time enough for that, forfooth Father, but
I have fuch a natural Affection for my Sifter, that me-
thinks I could live and die with her Give me thy
Hand, fweet Sifter
Sir John She's beholden to you, Sir
Sir Mart What if fhe be, Sir, what's that to you,
Sir ?
Sir John I hope, Sir, I have not offended you ?
Sir Mart It may be you have, and it may be you have
not, Sir , you fee I have no Mind to fatisfy you, Sir .
                                                What

What a Devil ' a Man cannot talk a little to his own Flesh and Blood, but you muſt be interpoſing with a Murrain to you

Mood Enough of this, good *Anthony*, this Gentleman is to marry your Siſter.

Sir *Mart* He marry my Siſter ' Ods foot, Sir, there are ſome Baſtards, that ſhall be nameleſs, that are as well worthy to marry her, as any Man, and have as good Blood in their Veins

Sir *John.* I do not queſtion it in the leaſt, Sir.

Sir *Mart.* 'Tis not your beſt Courſe, Sir; you marry my Siſter ' what have you ſeen of the World, Sir ? I have ſeen your Hurricanos, and your Calentures, and your E-clipticks, and your Tropick Lines, Sir, an you go to that, Sir

Warn. You muſt excuſe my Maſter, the Sea's a little working in his Brain, Sir

Sir *Mart.* And your *Preſter Johns* o'th' *Eaſt-Indies*, and your Great *Turk* of *Rome* and *Perſia*

Mood Lord, what a thing it is to be Learned, and a Traveller ' Bodikin, it makes me weep for Joy, but, *Anthony*, you muſt not bear your ſelf too much upon your Learning, Child

Mill Pray, Brother, be civil to this Gentleman for my ſake

Sir *Mart.* For your ſake, Siſter *Millifcent*, much may be done, and here I kiſs your Hand on't

Warn Yet again, Stupidity ?

Mill. Nay, pray Brother Hands off, now you are too rude.

Sir *Mart* Dear Siſter, as I am a true *Eaſt-India* Gentle-man ——

Mood But pray, Son *Anthony*, let us talk of other Matters ; and tell me truly, had you not quite forgot me ? And yet I made woundy much of you when you were young

Sir *Mart* I remember you as well as if I ſaw you but Yeſterday A fine grey-headed —— grey-bearded old Gentleman as ever I ſaw in all my Life.

Warn

Warn. Aside] Grey-bearded old Gentleman! when he was a Scholar at *Cambridge.*

Mood. But do you remember where you were bred up?

Sir Mart. O yes, Sir, moſt perfectly, in the Iſle——ſtay——let me ſee, oh——now I have it——in the Iſle of *Silly.*

Mood. In the Iſle of *Ely*, ſure you mean?

Warn Without doubt he did, Sir, but this damn'd Iſle of *Silly* runs in's Head ever ſince his Sea-Voyage.

Mood And your Mother's Name was——come, pray let me examine you——for that I'm ſure you cannot forget

Sir Mart Warner ! what was it, *Warner ?*

Warn Poor Mrs *Dorothy Draw-water*, if ſhe were now alive, what a joyful Day would this be to her?

Mood Who the Devil bid you ſpeak, Sirrah?

Sir Mart. Her Name, Sir, was Mrs *Dorothy Draw-water*

Sir John I'll be hang'd if this be not ſome Cheat

Mill. He makes ſo many ſtumbles, he muſt needs fall at laſt.

Mood But you remember, I hope, where you were born?

Warn Well, they may talk what they will of *Oxford* for an Univerſity, but *Cambridge* for my Money

Mood Hold your Tongue you Scanderbag Rogue you, this is the ſecond time you have been talking when you ſhould not

Sir Mart I was born at *Cambridge*, I remember it as perfectly as if it were but Yeſterday.

Warn How I ſweat for him ! he's remembring ever ſince he was born.

Mood And who did you go over with to the *Eaſt-Indies ?*

Sir Mart Warner !

Warn 'Twas a happy thing, Sir, you lighted upon ſo honeſt a Merchant as Mr *Bonaventure*, to take care of him.

Mood.

Mood. Sawcy Rafcal! this is paſt all Sufferance

Roſe We are undone, *Warner,* if this Diſcourſe go on any further.

Lord Pray, Sir, take pity o'th' poor Gentlemen, he has more need of a good Supper, than to be aſk'd ſo many Queſtions

Sir John. Theſe are Rogues, Sir, I plainly perceive it; pray let me aſk him one Queſtion —— Which way did you come home, Sir?

Sir Mart. We came home by Land, Sir.

Warn That is, from *India* to *Perſia,* from *Perſia* to *Turkey,* from *Turkey* to *Germany,* from *Germany* to *France*

Sir John. And from thence, over the narrow Seas on Horſe-back.

Mood 'Tis ſo, I diſcern it now, but ſome ſhall ſmoak for't Stay a little *Anthony,* I'll be with you preſently.
[*Exit* Mood.

Warn That wicked old Man is gone for no good, I'm afraid; would I were fairly quit of him. [*Aſide.*

Mill aſide] Tell me no more of Sir *Martin, Roſe,* he wants natural Senſe, to talk after this rate, but for this *Warner,* I am ſtrangely taken with him, how handſomely he brought him off!

Enter Moody *with two Cudgels*

Mood Among half a Score tough Cudgels I had in my Chamber, I have made choice of theſe two as beſt able to hold out

Mill Alas! poor *Warner* muſt be beaten now for all his Wit, would I could bear it for him

Warn But to what end is all this Preparation, Sir?

Mood In the firſt place, for your Worſhip, and in the next, for this *Eaſt-India* Apoſtle, that will needs be my Son *Anthony.*

Warn. Why d'ye think he is not?

Mood. No, thou wicked Accomplice in his Deſigns, I know he is not

VOL. II.   H   *Warn.*

Wurm. Who, I his Accomplice? I befeech you, Sir, what is it to me; if he fhould prove a Counterfeit! I affure you he has cozen'd me in the firft place.

Sir John. That's likely, i'faith, cozen his own Servant?

Warn As I hope for Mercy, Sir, I am an utter Stranger to him, he took me up but Yefterday, and told me the Story word for word as he told it you.

Sir Mart What will become of us two now? I truft to the Rogue's Wit to bring me off.

Mood If thou would'ft have me believe thee, take one of thefe two Cudgels, and help me to lay it on foundly.

Warn With all my Heart.

Mood Out you Cheat, you Hypocrite, you Impoftor. Do you come hither to cozen an honeft Man?

            [*Beats him*

Sir *Mart* Hold, hold, Sir!

Warn Do you come hither with a Lye to get a Father, Mr *Anthony* of *Eaft India?*

Sir *Mart* Hold, you inhuman Butcher.

Warn I'll teach you to counterfeit again, Sir.

Sir *Mart* The Rogue will murder me.

           [*Exit Sir Mart*

Mood A fair Riddance of 'em both. Let's in and laugh at 'em   [*Exeunt.*

   Enter again Sir Martin *and* Warner.

Sir *Mart* Was there ever fuch an Affront put upon a Man, to be beaten by his Servant.

Warn After my hearty Salutations upon your Backfide, Sir, may a Man have leave to afk you, what News from the *Mogul's* Country?

Sir *Mart* I wonder where thou hadft the Impudence to move fuch a Queftion to me, knowing how thou haft us'd me.

Warn Now, Sir, you may fee what comes of your Indifcretion and Stupidity I always gave you warning
                of

of it, but for this time I am content to pass it by without more Words, partly, because I have already corrected you, though not so much as you deserve

Sir Mart. Do'st thou think to carry it off at this rate, after such an Injury?

Warn You may thank your self for't; nay, 'twas very well I found out that way, otherwise I had been suspected as your Accomplice.

Sir Mart But you laid it on with such a Vengeance, as if you were beating of a Stock-fish.

Warn To confess the Truth on't, you had anger'd me, and I was willing to evaporate my Choler, if you will pass it by so, I may chance to help you to your Mistress No more Words of this Business, I advise you, but go home and grease your Back

Sir Mart. In fine, I must suffer it at his Hands: for if my Shoulders had not paid for this Fault, my Purse must have sweat Blood for't: The Rogue has got such a hank upon me ——

Warn. So, so! here's another of our Vessels come in after the Storm that parted us!

Enter Rose.

What Comfort, *Rose*, no Harbour near?

Rose My Lady, as you may well imagine, is most extreamly incens'd against Sir *Martin*, but she applauds your Ingenuity to the Skies I'll say no more, but thereby hangs a Tale

Sir Mart. I am considering with my self about a Plot, to bring all about again

Rose. Yet again plotting! if you have such a Mind to't, I know no way so proper for you, as to turn Poet to *Pugenello*

Warn. Hark! is not that Musick in your House?

[*Musick Plays*

Rose Yes, Sir *John* has given my Mistress the Fiddles, and our old Man is as jocund yonder, and does

H 2   so

fo hug himfelf to think how he has been reveng'd upon you

Warn. Why, he does not know 'twas we, I hope?

Rofe 'Tis all one for that

Sir Mart I have fuch a Plot; I care not, I will fpeak
an I were to be hang'd for't —— fhall I fpeak, dear
Warner? let me now, it does fo wamble within me,
juft like a Clyfter, i'faith law, and I can keep it no
longer for my Heart

Warn. Well, I am indulgent to you; out with it boldly
in the Name of Nonfenfe

Sir Mart. We two will put on Vizards, and with the
help of my *Landlord*, who fhall be of the Party, go a
Mumming there, and by fome device of dancing, get
my Miftrefs away unfufpected by 'em all

Rofe. What if this fhould hit now, when all your Projects have fail'd, *Warner?*

Warn. Would I were hang'd, if it be not fomewhat
probable Nay, now I confider better on't —— ex-
ceeding probable, it muft take, 'tis not in Nature to be
avoided

Sir Mart. O muft it fo, Sir' and, who may you thank
for't?

Warn. Now am I fo mad he fhould be the Author of
this Device. How the Devil, Sir, came you to ftumble
on't?

Sir Mart Why fhould not my Brains be as fruitful as
yours, or any Man's?

Warn This is fo good, it fhall not be your Plot, Sir,
either difown it, or I will proceed no further.

Sir Mart I would not lofe the Credit of my Plot to
gain my Miftrefs The Plot's a good one, and I'll juftify
it upon any Ground in *England*, an you will not work
upon't, it fhall be done without you

Rofe I think the Knight has Reafon.

Warner. Well, I'll order however to the beft Ad-
vantage· Hark you, *Rofe*   [*Whifpers.*

Sir Mart. If it mifcarry by your Ordering, take notice
'tis

'tis your Fault; 'tis well invented, I'll take my Oath on't.

Rose I muſt in to 'em, for fear I ſhould be ſuſpected; but I'll acquaint my Lord, my old Lady, and all the reſt who ought to know it, with your Deſign

Warn We'll be with you in a twinkling. You and I, *Roſe,* are to follow our Leaders, and be pur'd to Night ———

Roſe To have, and to hold, are dreadful Words, *Warner* ; but for your ſake I'll venture on 'em [*Exeunt*

Enter Lord, Lady Dupe, *and* Chriſtian.

L. *Dupe* Nay' good my Lord, be patient

Lord Does he think to give Fiddles and Treatments in a Houſe where he has wrong'd a Lady ? I'll never ſuffer it.

L *Dupe* But upon what ground will you raiſe your Quarrel ?

Lord A very juſt one, as I am her Kinſman

L *Dupe* He does not know yet why he was to be arreſted ; try that way again

Lord. I'll hear of nothing but Revenge.

Enter Roſe.

Roſe Yes, pray hear me one word, my Lord, Sir *Martin* himſelf has made a Plot.

Chr That's like to be a good one.

Roſe A Fool's Plot may be as lucky as a Fool's Hand ſel , 'tis a very likely one, and requires nothing for your part, but to get a Parſon in the next Room, we'll find work for him

L *Dupe.* That ſhall be done immediately, *Chriſtian,* make haſte, and ſend for Mr *Ball* the Non-conformiſt, tell him here are two or three Angels to be earn'd

Chr And two or three Poſſets to be eaten May I not put in that, Madam ?

L *Dupe* Surely you may [*Exit Ch ſtian.*

Rofe Then for the reft —— 'tis only this —— Oh!
they are here! pray take it in a whifper. My Lady
knows of it already.

Enter Moody, *Sir* John, *and* Millifent.

Mill. Strike up again, Fiddle, I'll have a *French*
Dance

Sir John. Let's have the Brawls

Mood. No, good Sir *John*, no quarrelling among
Friends

L Dupe Your Company is like to be increas'd, Sir,
fome Neighbours that heard your Fiddles are come a
mumming to you.

Mood Let 'em come in, and we'll be jovy; an I had
but my Hobby-horfe at home ————

Sir John What, are they Men or Women?

L Dupe I believe fome 'Prentices broke loofe.

Mill Rofe! go and fetch me down two *Indian* Gowns
and Vizard-masks —— you and I will difguife too,
and be as good a Mummery to them as they to us
　　　　　　　　　　　　　　　　　[*Exit* Rofe.

Mood. That will be moft rare

Enter Sir Martin Mar-all, Warner, *Landlord difguis'd like a Tony*

Mood O here they come! Gentlemen Maskers you are
welcome —— [Warner *figns to the Mufick for a Dance*]
He figns for a Dance I believe; you are welcome　Mr.
Mufick, ftrike up, I'll make one as old as I am

Sir John. And I'll not be out.　　　　　　[*Dance*

Lord Gentlemen-Maskers, you have had your Frolick, the next turn is mine; bring two Flute-glaffes and
fome Stools, ho, we'll have the Ladies Health.

Sir John But why Stools, my Lord?

Lord That you fhall fee　The Humour is, that two
Men at a time are hoifted up; when they are above,
they name their Ladies, and the reft of the Compa-
　　　　　　　　　　　　　　　　　　　　　　　ny

ny dance about them while they drink : This they call the Frolick of the Altitudes.

Mood Some Highlander's Invention, I'll warrant it.

Lord. Gentlemen-maskers, you shall begin

       [*They hoist Sir* Mart *and* Warn.

Sir John Name the Ladies.

Lord They point to Mrs *Millisent* and Mrs *Christian*. A Lou's Touche ! Touche !

     [*While they drink, the Company dances and sings :*
       They are taken down.

Mood A rare toping Health this Come, Sir *John*, now you and I will be in our Altitudes

Sir John What new Device is this, tro ?

Mood I know not what to make on't.

     [*When they are up,* [*the Company dances about 'em :*
      Then dance off. Tony *dances a Jigg*

Sir John Pray, Mr Fool, where's the rest o'your Company ? I would fain see 'em again   [*To* Tony.

Land Come down and tell 'em so, *Cudden.*

Sir John I'll be hang'd if there be not some Plot in't, and this Fool is set here to spin out the time.

Mood Like enough ! undone ! undone ! my Daughter's gone, let me down, Sirrah

Land Yes, *Cudden*

Sir John My Mistress is gone, let me down first.

Land This is the quickest way, *Cudden*

      [*He offers to pull down the Stools.*

Sir John. Hold ! hold ! or thou wilt break my Neck.

Land An you will not come down, you may stay there, *Cudden*   [*Exit Landlord dancing.*

Mood O Scanderbag Villains !

Sir John Is there no getting down ?

Mood All this was long of you, Sir *Jack.*

Sir John 'Twas long of your self to invite them hi-ther

Mood O you young Coxcomb, to be drawn in thus !

Sir John You old Sot you, to be caught so sillily !

Mood. Come but an Inch nearer, and I'll so claw thee.

         Sir *John.*

Sir *John* I hope I shall reach to thee

Mood An 'twere not for thy wooden Breast-work there ——

Sir *John* I hope to push thee down from *Babylon*.

Enter Lord, Lady Dupe, *Sir* Martin, Warner, Rose, Millisent veil'd, and Landlord

Lord. How, Gentlemen! what, quarrelling among your selves!

Mo..d Coxnowns! help me down, and let me have fair play, he shall never marry my Daughter

Sir *Mart* *leading Rose* No, I'll be sworn that he shall not, therefore never repine, Sir, for Marriages you know are made in Heav'n In fine, Sir, we are join'd together in spight of Fortune

Rose *pulling off her Mask* That we are indeed, Sir *Martin*, and these are Witnesses; therefore, in fine, never repine, Sir, for Marriages you know are made in Heav'n

Omn Rose!

Warn What is *Rose* split in two? Sure I ha' got one *Rose*!

Mill Ay, the best *Rose* you ever got in all your Life.

[*Pulls off her Mask.*

Warn This amazeth me so much, I know not what to say or think.

Mood My Daughter married to *Warner* !

Sir *Mart* Well, I thought it impossible any Man in *England* should have over-reach'd me; Sure *Warner* there was some Mistake in this. Pr'ythee *Billy* let's go to the Parson to set all right again, that every Man may have his own, before the matter go too far

Warn Well, Sir! for my part I will have nothing farther to do with these Women, for I find they will be too hard for us, but e'en sit down by the Loss, and content my self with my hard Fortune But, Madam, do you ever think I will forgive you this, to cheat me into an Estate of two thousand Pounds a Year?

Sir *Mart.*

Sir Mart An I were as thee, I would not be fo ferv'd, *Warner !*

Mill. I have ferv'd him but right for the Cheat he put upon me, when he perfuaded me you were a Wit —— now there's a Trick for your Trick, Sir.

Warn Nay, I confefs you have out-witted me.

Sir John. Let me down, and I'll forgive all freely.

[*They let him down.*

Mood. What am I kept here for ?

Warn I might in Policy keep you there, 'till your Daughter and I had been in private, for a little Confum-mation. But for once, Sir, I'll truft your good Nature

[*Takes him down too.*

Mood. An thou wert a Gentleman it would not grieve me !

Mill That I was affur'd of before I marry'd him, by my Lord here.

Lord. I cannot refufe to own him for my Kinfman, though his Father's Sufferings in the late Times have ruin'd his Fortunes.

Mood. But yet he has been a Serving-man.

Warn. You are miftaken, Sir, I have been a Mafter; and befides, there's an Eftate of eight hundred Pounds a Year, only it is mortgag'd for fix thoufand Pounds.

Mood Well, we'll bring it off; and for my part, I am glad my Daughter has mifs'd *in fine* there.

Sir John. I will not be the only Man that muft fleep without a Bedfellow to Night, if this Lady will once a-gain receive me

L Dupe She's yours, Sir.

Lord. And the fame Parfon, that did the former Exe-cution, is ftill in the next Chamber; what with Cawdles, Wine, and Quidding, which he has taken in abundance, I think he will be able to wheedle two more of you into Matrimony.

Mill. Poor *Sir Martin* looks melancholy ! I am half afraid he is in love.

Warn. Not with the Lady that took him for a Wit, I hope.

Rofe.

Rose At leaſt, Sir *Martin* can do more than you Mr. *Warner*, for he can make me a Lady, which you cannot my Miſtreſs

Sir Mart I have loſt nothing but my Man, and in fine, I ſhall get another

Mill. You'll do very well, Sir *Martin*, for you'll never be your own Man, I aſſure you

Warn For my part, I had lov'd you before, if I had follow'd my Inclination.

Mill But now I am afraid you begin of the lateſt, except your Love can grow up like a Muſhroom at a Night's warning.

Warn. For that matter never trouble your ſelf, I can love as faſt as any Man, when I am nigh Poſſeſſion ; my Love falls heavy, and never moves quick till it comes near the Center ; he's an ill Falconer that will unhood before the Quarry be in ſight.

Love's an high-mettl'd Hawk that beats the Air,
But ſoon grows weary when the Game's not near.

EPILOGUE.

AS Country Vicars, when the Sermon's done,
    Run huddling to the Benediction;
Well knowing, though the better sort may stay,
The vulgar Rout will run unblest away
So we, when once our Play is done, make haste
With a short Epilogue to close your Taste.
In thus withdrawing we seem mannerly,
But when the Curtain's down, we peep and see
A Jury of the Wits, who still stay late,
And in their Club decree the poor Play's Fate,
Then Verdict back is to the Boxes brought,
Thence all the Town pronounces it their Thought.
Thus, Gallants, we like Lilly can foresee,
But if you ask us what our Doom will be,
We by to Morrow will our Fortune cast,
As he tells all things when the Year is past.

Lightning Source UK Ltd.
Milton Keynes UK
UKOW022053120313

207544UK00011B/619/P